The Elixir of Mystical Experience (Amrutanubhava)

I0085041

Milind Dhond MD

This book is dedicated to
Nivrittinath, the Guru's Guru,
Swami Radhikananda Saraswati
And Bapu.

Contents

Foreword by Swami Radhikananda Saraswati

| | SudGurunath Maharaj Ki Jai | |
| | Mahayogi Swamy Umananda Saraswati Ki Jai | |

In this work, Dr. Milind Dhond has done a great service to Shri Nivrittinath, a Guru and guide of Shri Dnyanadev. The world has always spoken highly of Shri Dnyanadev, as indeed he deserves, but very little is said about Shri Nivrittinath, who initiated Shri Dnyanadev on his spiritual path.

The author has managed to read *Amrutanubhava*, the original philosophical text, and weave it into a story that presents the esoteric aspects of the original work with clarity. "Nivritti" means one who retires or has detached himself from Samsara, or worldly life. In the story the author has based Nivritti on biographical elements from his own life, but has also included elements of the historical Nivritti's life. In doing so he pays homage to the guru of Dnyanadev. The author has introduced Shri Dnyaneshwar as Shri Nivritti's friend, where in reality the two were brothers. But this individual approach is harmless.

In his pursuit of enlightenment Nivritti meets the seven saints (Sapta Rishi) that follow the outline of original chapters in Amrutanubhava.

1. Lord Shiva - Shakti
2. Guru Shri Gahininath
3. Vani Guru
4. Dnyana - Pure knowledge
5. Sat-Chit-Anand
6. Shabda Guru
7. Ajnana - Ignorance

In the story, all have been personified as characters and the author has described Lord Shiva, Shakti, Guru, Pure knowledge, Ignorance, Shabda, and Sat Chit Anand in a very clear and simplified manner. The spiritual seeker should read this text.

The author introduces the concept of the Guru and initiation in the text. He ends it with Shri Dnyanadev being initiated with a Dhiksha, which is the first step in introduction to the spiritual world. Dhiksha is a process of imparting benevolent energy and kindling the lamp of knowledge in the disciple.

Finally, the entire journey culminates in Shri Nivrittinatha's enlightened state.

I must say the author has done a remarkable job and I would recommend the book for those who wish to attain a state of enlightenment or understand the finer elements of *Amrutanubhava*.

I congratulate Milind Dhond, with blessings for the book's success in revealing Truth to the seeker. It is an excellent work.

Swami Radhikananda Saraswati, Sidha Yoga School, Pune, India

April 2017

Preface

The original *Amrutanubhava* was written by the thirteenth century Marathi mystic Sant Jnaneshwar. Jnaneshwar is a wellknown saint in the state of Maharastra in India and has a large temple dedicated to him at the site of his maha-samadhi in Alandi, near Pune, India. This is the act of leaving one's body to merge back with the divine. He was born in 1271 and wrote his most famous work, *Dynaneshwari*, at the age of nineteen. This work is a treatise on the Bhagavad Gita and also throws light on Kundalini yoga. The following year he wrote *Amrutanubhava*, which is a work describing the Lord as if he were talking about himself. The work contains many mystical references and metaphors and is difficult to interpret and understand.I first read *Amrutanubhava* in 1998 but was unable to understand the spiritual knowledge contained within it. I have re-read the text every few years and with each subsequent reading have understood a little more of the message Jnaneshwar was trying to convey. This is in part due to my own spiritual progress through those years. I have presented the philosophical work as a story with the main character Nivritti, who historically is Jnaneshwar's older brother. The story is set in modern day rural India. The main character, Nivritti, is largely autobiographical and is not meant to be an accurate historical description of Jnaneshwar's older brother. The character flaws described are primarily my own!

The character of Bapu represents my own father who studied the works of Jnaneshwar in his younger days but later suffered from the debt of old age. The phrase "God is Jnana" crossed his lips once while we were sitting together, arising spontaneously from his silence. The village of Gondyala is the actual village where he was raised as a poor rural farmer. The other places described, are based on places I have visited, including Brahmana, where the banyan tree cathedral encompasses the palpable Chaitanya, or spiritual energy of a former sage's wisdom. I have visited the ancient ruined temple in the jungle with the carving of the Lord's feet. The experiences portrayed are also semi-autobiographical and are described to the reader to show how spiritual knowledge gradually changes the seeker. In the story I have paid homage to Nivritti, Jnaneshwar's brother and guru, by including events that occurred in his life. These include the episode of escaping from the tiger and his subsequent meeting with his own guru Gahininath. In the story I have made the two friends rather than brothers, but as previously stated this is not meant to be a biography of Nivritti or Jnaneshwar. The story is a vehicle for presenting the knowledge of *Amrutanubhava*. Below, I have outlined the esoteric aspects described in the story so that the uninitiated reader may understand the deeper meaning of the references.

Introduction

Following the introduction of Nivritti, I have followed Jnaneshwar's *Amrutanubhava*, which begins with a description of Shiva, the unmanifest divinity, and discusses the creation of the manifest universe and the role of Shakti and her relationship to Shiva. I have described Shiva and Shakti as husband and wife, describing their roles and how the manifestation of creation necessitates the creation of a duality. I have described Shiva as blue, representing the "color" of pure consciousness, and his breath signifying the creation and dissolution of the manifest universe along with the Ham-Sah mantra. This is the mantra that naturally occurs with each breath. The inhalation is the *Haa* component, the *mm* is the suspension, and the exhalation is the *Sah* component. This mantra allows the individual the ability to keep a meditative state during any activity, as breath is an essential part of worldly existence. The spanda or pulsation that Nivritti experiences in Shiva's presence is the underlying spanda that one experiences in deep meditation, while the vibration from the drum indicates the unstruck sound and vibration (anhaat naad) that occurs when the kundalini rises to the heart chakra. Shiva and Shakti are never together in the story due to the fact that Shiva and Shakti are artificially two separate entities but in reality one and the same. Hence with their union the duality ceases and also the creation, as this is only possible where duality is present. This same duality is playing out on both a cosmic scale and also in the individual being, where the Shakti is the Kundalini at the base of the spine and the Shiva is the Sahastrar at the top of the head. The objective in "achieving enlightenment" is to have the Kundalini rise to unite with the Shiva, thus allowing the individual to see his true non-dual infinite nature. In chapter two I then go on to describe the need for a guru on the path to enlightenment. This chapter contains aspects of how Nivritti himself came upon his own guru Gahininath and his subsequent initiation into spiritual life. This is a key component in spiritual evolution and often a contentious issue both in India and the West. The presence of fake gurus or the idea that a mortal individual can manifest the divine are often cited as reasons to doubt the validity of the guru-disciple (shishya) relationship. The true seeker should not expend energy worrying about things that detract from the search for truth. The true guru will always find the seeker, who will intuitively know in their heart their guru's presence. "The teacher will appear when the student is ready" is the most apt phrase to highlight how a guru will appear before the seeker. It highlights the need for sincere effort and a burning desire to experience the Truth. Gahininath initiates Nivritti with a shaktipat diksha and transmits spiritual knowledge directly into him. This practice is thousands of years old and is how true knowledge is maintained in the world today. It is always a person-to-person transmission, guru to student. The level of the transmission is related primarily to the receptiveness of the student to receiving the diksha. The guru, acting as a lightning rod, channels divine energy into the student. I have described Nivritti's diksha experience as one of astral travel, which can be experienced by meditation on the Manipura chakra. The guru also explains the universe in terms of a blank canvas, which I have found useful when trying to describe the relationship of the divine to creation. He then describes the chakras and the process of spiritual unfolding that occurs as the Kundalini rises. Chapter three, Vani guru, starts with Nivritti passing a banyan tree on which are perched three birds busily engaging in worldly activities while on a separate branch another is quietly watching. This is an analogy that Jnaneshwar himself uses to convey the four states of consciousness. In their meeting Vani describes the meaning of the Om symbol as representing the three states of consciousness: awake, dreaming, and deep sleep. He also describes the fourth state, or Turiya, which is the foundational consciousness on which the other three are overlaid. I have included a wonderful description of this state from the Kena Upanishad,"the ear of the ear," which helps to crystallize the essence of Turiya. They then meditate on the Ajna chakra located in the middle of the forehead between the eyes, and the mudra and seed mantra are outlined. Prior to the meditation Vani guru instructs Nivritti on invoking blessings on the lineage through which this spiritual knowledge has been passed down. Nivritti then salutes the Sad-guru, which is the guru within him, as well as his own guru, Gahininath, and Vani guru. Since spiritual knowledge is transmitted from guru to student, every meditation always begins with this salutation. This is not just a perfunctory gesture but in fact sets off a cascade of spiritual energy, as those who follow this practice well know. The salutation and the seed mantra and mudra for Ajna chakra meditation are included so that the reader can practice for themselves. At the end of the meditation with Vani, Nivritti experiences a state of Ananda, or bliss. This state is not "attained" by meditation but rather is one's own essential nature that is revealed in the silence. The seeker should try and achieve this level of silence and depth in their regular meditation. The chapter also deals with the importance of sound and the four levels of speech. It outlines how prior to any speech the thought of what is to be said starts in the silence, or Para level of existence. This is at the level of the divine. At this point even the seed of the thought does not exist as separate from divinity. An arc of descent then occurs as the thought descends to the seed level and then develops duality as it comes into one's mind at the madhyama level. The thought is then spoken verbally at the vaikhari level. This highlights the need for great care with speech and the use of words. It also shows how one can ascend the arc back to the divine. The chapter ends with Vani uttering "great words" or a mahavakhya. These are phrases, traditionally in Sanskrit, that contain pointers to the divine. The mahavakhya I have used, "Akanda mandalakaram," is from the text Guru Gita which praises the Guru and throws light on the same subject. Pure knowledge (Jnana) outlines the use and limitations of words in trying to know the truth and reaching a state of perfection. The Pure knowledge is represented by a sage that appears in Nivritti's inner vision. He uses allegory and metaphors such as the moon and its eclipse to try and illuminate the nature of Jnana to the seeker. These are as described by Jnaneshwar in the original work. He also talks about how anything in the world of opposites is not the truth. Happiness and sadness, wealth and poverty, and all other opposites will not lead to enlightenment. This also applies to knowledge and ignorance. Relative knowledge consists of names and forms and cannot lead to the truth. Jnaneshwar's own description is of the flame of knowledge burning the camphor of ignorance, but in the end, as in the realm of the truth, both will be extinguished. The sage then goes on to talk about the concept of the seer, seen, and seeing trio that is our existence. The individual views the world as if he is the subject and everything around is the object, which is not the reality. The truth is where there is no subject-object difference and the only thing is the process of seeing. The best way of realizing this is when gazing in a mirror. The subject and object are the same and only the seeing aspect is occurring. This is the divine vision of the world for the enlightened, where the seer and the seen are viewed as part of the divine consciousness where the concept of duality is no more. The sage goes on to describe the methods by which the seeker can achieve this vision of the world. They include meditation on mantra, concentrating on the silence between thoughts, and also in transition points of consciousness: These are the moments when transitioning from sleep to wakefulness, and vice versa, where the individual can experience the Turiya state. He also talks of the technique of dropping all past and future thoughts and holding oneself in the present moment. This technique has gained a lot of traction in the West as "mindfulness." The Sat, Chit, Ananda chapter deals with the classical description of God as existence, consciousness, and bliss. These words are meant to be a pointer to the truth and are to be understood intuitively, not literally.

The words are not separate and distinct aspects of the divine but together fundamentally represent the whole. Existence also represents the unmanifest form of the divine, or the blank canvas in the painting analogy. The consciousness has the potential for manifestation, or painting creation on the canvas, while the bliss aspect is the nature of the canvas and painting itself. Nivritti walks through the village and comes across a man with wheat seeds and in his inner vision sees the flour and tastes the bread. He also sees a woman stringing a veena and can hear the music. These are examples used by Jnaneshwar to explain the unmanifest and manifest aspects of the divine. The flour and the bread already exist in an unmanifest state in the wheat. In the painting analogy the wheat is on the painting while the flour and bread are on the blank canvas waiting to be painted. This is also true for the music that Nivritti hears. All things that will ever exist in the manifest universe already exist in an unmanifest state. Meditation and connecting to the silence will allow the individual access to the unmanifest state and allow the unlocking of creative, artistic, and intellectual abilities that would otherwise not be possible. Nivritti also comes across a man trying to measure his height by using his shadow. The analogy used by Jnaneshwar shows the absurdity of trying to use the reflection of the divine to understand the divine itself. He is then shown several meditation techniques in detail that are taken from the text of my first book, *Journey to Zero*. The techniques are from the original text Vijnana Bhairava, which outlines 112 meditations for achieving enlightenment. Several of these are included in detail for the reader's practice. The concept of Shunya, or void, is touched upon. This is the point described in other spiritual writings such as St John of the cross where the seeker has to traverse a place of nonexistence. This is the transition point from where the path for the Kundalini ends in the Ajna chakra and has to pass to the Sahastrar. I think it is best described as entering the dark-less dark before reaching the lightless light. Meditation on the void represents a more advanced form of meditation for the seasoned seeker. In the book, Nivritti's spiritual evolution occurs very quickly, but the seeker may find the whole process takes many years. The chapter on Shabda guru looks at the usefulness of words and their ultimate failure in realizing the truth. I have made Shabda guru blind to try and highlight this point. The use of words keeps the individual in the realm of name and form and cannot ultimately lead to enlightenment. If this were not true then the words that lead one to enlightenment would already have been written. The guru tries to show Nivritti, by examples, how the idea of words removing ignorance is a fallacy, since we have already seen that the ignorance itself is non-existent. In the light of true knowledge, just as in the light of the sun, the importance of the lamp of words is irrelevant and of no use. The analogy of ignorance as the shadow and the blue sky are used by Jnaneshwar himself. The perception that the shadow or the blueness of the sky are real, is itself the fallacy and therefore words cannot remove something that is not really there. In the light of true knowledge the shadow and the blueness are seen for what they are-not real. Words, therefore, make no difference. Shabda guru then goes on to explain the progression and final destination of the enlightened person. He describes the process of seeing with no seer or object seen, and the ability of the enlightened person to withdraw this seeing element and have sentiency only — the state of Nirvikalpa Samadhi. The chapter on Ajnana, or ignorance, is the longest chapter in Jnaneshwar's book and outlines the fact that ignorance belongs firmly in the realm of name and form. The Ajnana character I have described represents the arrogance and hubris of one filled with worldly knowledge who does not perceive the divinity. He is busily engaged in futile worldly tasks such as creating the salt fish, which is an analogy that Jnaneshwar himself uses. Ajnana's perception of the world, such as his fear of the snake in the tree, is shown to be due to ignorance about the true nature of the snake being that of an old rope. The same is true for us in our own worldly lives, and part of spiritual development is changing one's perspective. Since ignorance does not exist in the divine realm, I have Ajnana disappear on the arrival of the guru. Gahininath then proceeds to reinforce in Nivritti the need to see beyond the world of opposites and uses the wave on the ocean and sunlight as examples, again as Jnaneshwar does in the original work. The wave is the individual life perceived as being separate from the ocean, but in reality the ocean and the wave are both made of the water of divine consciousness. Similarly, the sunlight is dark and things are seen because of the reflection of the divine consciousness. If a cloud covers the sun and there is perceived darkness, it is precisely because of the sunlight that the cloud is seen in the first place. Neither the darkness nor the reflected light have any relevance in the realm of the sun. So it is true with divine consciousness. What we see as good or bad, happy or sad is all relative. They are all illuminated by the underlying bliss of consciousness. That is to be realized by the seeker in moments of happiness and also in sorrow. The underlying bliss of one's existence is still the same in both these states. The guru describes yoga bhumika, or gaps in the worldly life where the underlying divine consciousness is most prevalent and thus easier to perceive.

The chapter concludes with the river becoming a raging ocean representing worldly life, or Samsara. This relates to a salutation to the guru I have read, where the disciple praised the guru for leading them across the ocean of Samsara but on reaching the other side gazed back and realized both the ocean and the guru were nonexistent! Finally, the work ends by describing the nature of one who has transcended worldly existence, Jivan Mukta, and lives life as an enlightened individual. It shows how a gradual process of enlightenment occurs and that Nivritti is now firmly on that path. The spiritual seeker is not exempt from bad events that occur in Samsara, but rather accepts them as part of the divine play and does not allow them to disturb the tranquility of his mind. He is at his uncle's funeral and sees the sorrow of the people around him, yet is able to connect to his underlying divine blissful nature. He has the same experience when passing the funeral home. I go on to describe how he overcomes anger, the most destructive emotion, by making his mind one-pointed in the moment and thus also dissolving it into bliss. This technique is also described in *Journey to Zero*. The importance of listening to intuitive knowledge and following it when it arises is touched upon when Nivritti buys the jillibee, not knowing why he is doing it at the time. He meets the beggar, who transforms into Lord Shiva and subsequently into his own guru. This highlights how the Lord manifests everywhere as everything, which is ultimately the vision of the enlightened person. Gahininath instructs him to live his life relying on intuitive knowledge, or Jnana. "God is Jnana," as stated by my father, and the guru indeed epitomizes what the view of the world needs to be. The blue pearl of pure consciousness is mentioned as a marker of a highly evolved state of enlightenment. It begins initially as a black dot that darts around in meditation and over time develops into a black pearl. This eventually becomes a deep blue opalescent color seen in the heart in intense meditation.

The characters in the book are fictional and not meant to represent an accurate biography of Nivritti and his brother Jnaneshwar. I finish the book by having Nivritti initiate Jnaneshwar, which is historically accurate. The book is intended as a vehicle to understand the knowledge contained in Jnaneshwar's great work *Amrutanubava*. In making him the main character I have paid homage to Nivritti, the guru's guru.

Acknowledgements

I have used translations of *Amrutanubhava* from three sources: Swami Radhikananda Saraswati from the Sidha Yoga school in Pune India, Swami Anubhavananda, and Swami Abhayananda, the latter of which is available online as a PDF. Since any spiritual undertaking is also about expanding on the original work, I have taken the liberty of adding knowledge from the Upanishads and also describe techniques of meditation that appear in my first book, *Journey to Zero*. This is a self-authored book containing techniques for enlightenment outlined in the mystical work Vijnana Bhairava.

This work would not be possible without the grace of my own guru Swami Radhikananda, whose counselling and spiritual instruction have guided me on this path. I humbly offer this work at her feet.

Milind Dhond (March 2017)

The Elixir of Mystical Experience

Nivritti

Nivritti was born in Gondyala, a small village situated near the Konkan mountains, in the state of Maharashtra, India. He belonged to a poor Brahmin family that had lived there for several centuries, primarily as subsistence farmers. Now in his late teens, he lived in a small clay hut with his maternal aunt and uncle. He had been orphaned at the age of twelve with his mother's death, his father having died some years previously. He had cultivated a jovial and happy demeanor for himself amongst the other villagers and now in his late teens was a wiry, thin, and handsome boy. The jovial nature and happy-go-lucky image he had inculcated belied a dark melancholy that had been with him since his mother's death. It was something from which he could not escape. Rukmini, his elderly aunt, lived with her husband Bapu in a small hut at the edge of the village. Bapu had been a postmaster in the local town of Kudal but was now retired. He had been an intellectual man, versed in the ancient Indian scriptures and texts. In the light of his younger days people from the village would gather to hear him recite the poetry of the great spiritual works such as the Bhagavad Gita or the Vedas. He was able to quote the sacred verses in both the original Sanskrit and in the local dialect, Marathi. The villagers would always plead for his poetry, and like some Vedic pied piper, they would listen as if spellbound by some magical force. He had a deep melodic voice and had mastered the rhyme and meter of those ancient poems. He had developed pride in his ability and it had heightened his standing in the village. In this world, spiritual knowledge was considered a great prize, more so than money or intellectual knowledge. The poor villagers equated Bapu's ability to recite these verses as on a par with the great Sage composers themselves. However, the light of Bapu's intellect had long since faded and he was prone to bouts of confusion and rumination. Most of the time he sat in silence, gazing towards an unknown horizon. The doctors could find no organic illness and it had been put down to aging and dementia. Every so often the light would shine bright and he would quote a verse or two, but these instances were fewer and fewer. They had no children of their own, but for the past five years had looked after Rukmini's sister's only son Nivritti. Nivritti had been a godsend to Rukmini, who was having more and more difficulty with her husband as he declined both mentally and physically. Nivritti would help with bathing and dressing Bapu, which was increasingly difficult for her slight frame. He also helped with carrying rice and vegetables from Kudal, where they would go weekly. He was also good company for her since Bapu's mental decline. In the evenings, as Bapu would sit gazing across the rice paddocks in silence, Nivritti would sit beside him and gently hold his hand. The old man would smile and in his silent prison, dream of past glory. Like most of his classmates, Nivritti had left school at sixteen. Higher education was a luxury that he and his friends could not afford. The young men's ability to earn, meager as it was, allowed their families to fend off starvation. Nivritti's day began early, as Bapu was an early riser and had to be given his tea and have his morning bath. He would take the old man to the well and stand him on a rock a few feet away. He would then use the lever to lower a large iron pot into the well. The pot was secured tightly to the bamboo lever with rope. Once the pot was nearly full he would lean back on the end of the large bamboo stick and lever it out. He would hand his uncle a bar of soap and using a small earthen pot would pour the cold water over his uncle's head. Again and again he would fill and pour until the soap was all washed out. He could see his uncle shiver as the cold water flowed over his head. It seemed to wake him from his stupor and he would start mumbling something about stamp duty or foreign mail. Following his own tea, Nivritti would cycle along a dirt red road past the other village houses, often greeting his neighbors along the way. Finally he would reach the paved road that led to Kudal. Here he would meet his childhood friend Jnanesh. They would race the first mile or so to a row of shops along the road where you could buy tea or Parle-G biscuits. They were largely wooden trolleys with corrugated iron roof and a makeshift cooker or kettle, but the tea they served was delicious and sweet. After that the two friends would make their way to Sarabagh, a small town two miles further down the road to Kudal on the banks of a tributary of the Panji river. The town was situated in a natural curve of the river that had widened into effectively a little bay and must have been a small port in earlier days. The town had about two or three hundred houses, most of which were brick or mortar, and had been an administrative stop in the days of British rule. The town was long past its prime but still had numerous shops, a hotel, dispensary and a crematorium. It had been Nivritti's mother's final port of call five years before. For Nivritti the smoke from the wooden pyres seemed to engulf the town in a haze of despair and gloom and on some days cast a shade so that even the sun appeared as a dark orange glow. Nivritti and Jnanesh would cycle past an old beggar that always sat on the corner of the building they worked in. He was dressed in filthy rags and covered in dirt which created such a foul odor that the boys could smell as they cycled past him. For some reason he knew Nivritti's name and would always call out to him as he flew past. "Nivritti, where is my dakshina?" he would call out. Nivritti knew the taunt of the term dakshina. It was a gift given to a spiritual guide. He knew the old fool was a beggar trying to get some money from him by appealing to his spiritual side, but the only dakshina the old beggar received was Nivritti's silent resentment. He and Jnanesh worked for the local Dhobi wala or washerman. His name was Santosh and he employed several washerwomen who would beat out the wet clothes on the rocks upriver with soap and then hang them up to dry. Drying clothes in the sweltering dry heat did not take long and Santosh employed several local boys to iron them all. On an average day they would iron two hundred or so clothes each. Santosh was a good businessman and had clients from all the local villages and the town itself. Santosh himself was a slightly portly fellow not adverse to sweet jillibees, ladoos and other Indian sweets that he seemed to consume on a daily basis and which had given him a small potbelly. Along with his receding hairline it aged him more than his actual years. He was a traditional Indian and would wear a long cotton loin cloth or dhoti instead of trousers as was now the custom. As he employed six staff he also fancied himself the local tycoon, though their combined salaries would not equal a bank teller's in Kudal. He believed in the traditions of the old Indian way of life and was a great follower of Gandhi. Since he was doing well financially he had set up a side business of distributing clothes and alms to the poor and needy of the surrounding villages. Nivritti and Jnanesh worked to sort out all the clothes and alms for distribution to the poor. After collecting the items they would travel to the surrounding villages and give out food and clothes. The work was hard but gave the boys a sense of purpose. Santosh was a fair and congenial boss to work for and he liked Nivritti and Jnanesh, who worked hard to do a good job. Jnanesh was deeply into worship of the Hindu gods and would go to the temple every day. He was like most Indians who viewed spirituality as a normal part of life, and the idea of not doing daily worship did not even occur to him, let alone the idea that there might be no god at all. He had an implicit faith and would always begin sentences with "If Bhagwan wishes it…" Nivritti, on the other hand, had lost his faith. It had burned on his mother's funeral pyre five years earlier and was consumed totally. There was no longer the sturdy wooden framed pyre of belief but instead the ashes of doubt. They were blown by the wind and had disappeared completely or left small ash marks here and there. How could there be a loving benevolent god when he had endured so much pain? He could not dispel the sorrow of his mother's loss. It hung onto him as if she herself were tugging at his clothes. It had not diminished in the years since her death. He had put on a façade because people don't like to be in the company of the morose. He had cultivated a jovial sense about him, asking people about their pursuits and family. He feigned interest in their mundane boring lives so they wouldn't ask him about his. When they did he would make some joke or other, since they didn't care about him anyway. The only person that truly loved him was gone. Nivritti also had an unseen side that rarely came out. A simmering rage had manifested itself out of his grief. He could not say from where this anger arose, but he had it. Anger at his loss, anger that the world was so unkind and that no one truly loved him. This emotion he had kept secret just like his grief. He did not allow it to surface, but it appeared subtly on his face when irritated. It was an imperceptible change in his look or smile, only noticeable to his one friend Jnanesh.

His daily routine too was gradually becoming unbearable. Every day he would cycle past the crematorium on his way to the Dhobiwala and he could smell the smoke from the pyres behind the ten foot high brick walls. It would create a void in his lower stomach and he would be gripped by weakness and terror. The feelings were always fleeting, but they occurred daily. He would see the devotees on the riverbank casting off the ashes of their loved ones with a priest reciting incantations.

"Your mother, father, husband, wife, whomever, is gone. They are gone and all your belief is not going to bring them back," he thought. There was a futility to it. Did they know for sure that their relative was in heaven? Did the priest who had dedicated his whole life to god know any more than they did? It was all ritual, meaningless, and ultimately amounted to nothing. Nobody knew the truth, nobody.

"Have you heard of the seven sages?" Jnanesh asked. He was sipping tea in Sarabagh, his head leaning forward over his glass cup as he blew into it. The hot steam covered his glasses with each breath and would then evaporate as quickly.

"No." Nivritti looked up at Jnanesh. He could sense by the tone of the question that Jnanesh was pondering deeply. He seemed hesitant, as if he were unsure of how to proceed.

"The seven sages are said to live in the jungles around the Konkan mountains and are supposed to bestow knowledge of the divine on those who are true seekers". Jnanesh paused. "My grandfather told me about someone from his village who went in search of them and returned in an enlightened state. "My friend, I cannot bear to see the grief in you, though you hide it well. I know you don't believe in my temple gods and all the rituals and pujas we do, so I am telling you this so that you can find some peace. What have you got to lose?"

Nivritti was silent. He could feel the anger and resentment rising within himself as if his inner secret had just been announced to the world. Yet he also knew that his friend was only trying to help him. He sat sipping the tea, gazing into the cup. The silence continued. "We'd better get back to Dhobiwala or he'll have finished off that jar of Ladoos he got yesterday," said Nivritti with a false smile and he poured out the last drops of tea. They headed back to work, still in awkward silence. However the seed of what he must do was planted and from then on, Nivritti could not stop thinking about it. Every Sunday Nivritti would take his uncle for a walk to a small shrine about a mile from their hut. It was a holy site that the villagers termed Brahmana. Across the other side of the paddy fields was a small hill about 30 feet high, and on it was a large banyan tree. It was hundreds of years old and was thought to be the site of a sage's Samadhi. This was a place where the sage had sat to meditate and left his body to unite with the divine. The ancient sage's body was supposedly under the banyan tree. The old man had faith that it was anyway. The banyan tree had, over the years, developed large branches coming over the top of the hill to the ground, creating a natural cathedral. It was nice and shaded there. A small shrine had been built under the tree's arches and his uncle offered some flowers. Nivritti squatted down in the shade and waited for the old man to finish. "This place has Chaitanya, do you feel it, Nivritti?" Bapu was lucid. "Do you feel it?" he repeated. Nivritti gazed up at his uncle, unsure of what to say.

"Uncle, what is Chaitanya?" said Nivritti

"Spiritual energy from a great soul… leaves some residue behind," muttered Bapu.

Nivritti did not know what to say. He wanted to ask his uncle more but was not used to talking much to him since he was rarely lucid and then only for very short periods.

"I have heard about the seven sages that live in the Konkan mountains, Uncle," said Nivritti. He paused but his uncle was silently gazing up at the tree arches.

"I want to go there, I want to know the truth. I want to know if they can show me god."

Bapu was silent, as if he had withdrawn back into his internal world.

They sat in silence for the next ten or fifteen minutes. Nivritti looked at the old man as he gazed at the arches. He wondered how much the old man really knew or could even remember. Nivritti finally broke the silence "Shall we go back home?"

"I can't, not yet, I have some mail to deliver to Kudal before the train leaves," said Bapu.

"You retired from the Postmaster job years ago, Uncle. You retired, remember?" said Nivritti.

He walk over and gently grasped his uncle's hand and started leading him out of the cathedral.

Bapu gazed at him. "If you don't see the sages you will never know," he muttered.

'Know what, Uncle?" said Nivritti

"God is Jnana," said Bapu.

Then Bapu looked at the ground and started humming. Nivritti looked at the old man for a second and wondered what the phrase meant. He felt a sense of relief that the old man had at least listened, understood, and in some small way offered some endorsement to his plan. The two men walked back slowly through the paddy field.

Lord Shiva and his wife Shakti

It had been two days since Nivritti had left the villagers of Gaokwod at the edge of the Konkan jungles. He was not used to travelling in the thick dense brush, let alone sleeping in it, especially not alone. The noises of all the animals, especially the insects at night chirping and buzzing around made him uneasy, but at least he was not truly alone!

The idea now seemed to be foolish, almost preposterous. Seven sages living in the jungle imparting knowledge of the Truth; he of all people knew that this was a journey of faith, a quality in which he was lacking. Or so he thought.

He had felt an inner urge to go, starting the moment that the words crossed Jnanesh's lips, he had known it. He was compelled.

He had now come across a particularly dense part of the forest and was cutting through the vines with a Koita, a half sword with a sharp blade that the villagers used to cut coconuts off the trees. He had been cutting for several minutes and was getting tired, his clothes now drenched in sweat and the jungle's humidity.

He could see a little clearing ahead as he hacked through the last few vines and leaves. Finally, he emerged into the small clearing. He felt a strange sensation come over him, like nothing he had experienced before. It was the feeling of silence. Ahead of him was a deer, standing completely transfixed, gazing across the clearing. He noticed that the animal noises had all gone silent and the jungle was quiet.

At the other side of the clearing he could make out someone sitting. He slowly approached. All about him the silence continued unabated.

A sage was sitting in the lotus position atop a tiger skin mat, his eyes partially closed, just a small slit remaining open. He had matted hair that flowed across his shoulders on both sides. On his head, the hair was matted in a cylindrical manner, creating something like a crown. At the top of the crown Nivritti noticed something moving. It was a cobra, its head and upper torso fanned out over the sage's head, protecting his face from the sunlight. The snake appeared to be in a trance-like state.

The sage's body seemed to be made of light and had a bluish hue to it. It was adorned with whitish grey markings of ash. There were three horizontal stripes on his forehead and across it the white ash had taken the form of a half moon. He also appeared to have ten arms. By the side of the sage was a small water pot or kammandalu and a small drum or damaru. Nivritti's heart started to pound, faster and faster. Even he, the non-believer, knew that Lord Shiva was before him.

Nivritti stood completely still, not wishing to make any noise that might disturb the great sage. A long period of time passed and still he remained motionless. All around the jungle maintained its silence.

As he watched, Nivritti could see the breath moving in and out of the great sage. He could make out a faint sound of "Ha" as he inhaled and "sa" as he exhaled. A subtle haze of water vapor would appear as he breathed out and it appeared to be sucked back in as he inhaled. The whole process of inhalation and exhalation had a rhythmic quality to it as the divine breath appeared as the vapor and was then reabsorbed back into the great sage. It felt like a gentle pulsation or throb and as Nivritti stood observing, his mind fell completely silent and he could make out the throb coming from within himself.

He gazed at the small drum by the sage's side and could make out a vibration coming from it — but there was nothing striking it to create the vibration.

Finally the great sage opened his eyes and placed one of his right arms on a yogadanda, a Y shaped staff that allowed him to rest his arm horizontally by his side. As he did so Nivritti noticed the breath from his nostrils change very slightly. He could now see that the vapor was emerging from both nostrils equally.

The sage gestured for Nivritti to approach. "Nivritti, what is it that you seek?" said the sage. At first Nivritti was a little startled that the sage should know his name, but he noticed that the light around his face brightened as he spoke. Nivritti bowed his head before the great being and falteringly tried to find the words to ask for what he wanted. In the great sage's presence his mind had become still like the forest.

"I wish to know the Truth, oh great sage," said Nivritti bending his head forward in a low bow. He continued, "I wish to experience the direct, immediate… err… realization of the divine. I have travelled here so that I may gain this knowledge."

The sage gazed at him and again his face shone brighter as he spoke "Nivritti, the Truth cannot be known."

He smiled. "It is beyond the known and the unknown."

Nivritti's heart sank, yet he persisted.

"I wish to know the nature of god, Oh great sage, for I am far from this knowledge."

The sage was silent for a moment.

"Nivritti, you have come here to seek the Truth and stand before me asking for that knowledge to be revealed to you.

"Your two eyes gaze upon my one image and your two lips speak with one voice, yet you claim you are far from this knowledge. The Truth is self-evident, it needs no clarification, it cannot be known by any other means. Each person seeking the Truth has to make the spiritual journey to realize this themselves, but do not fret, I will help you on your journey."

"It is getting late, Nivritti. You should make your way to my ashram," the sage continued.

"The ashram is a wonderful place, peaceful and blissful. It is tended to by my wife Shakti. She runs the household and allows all the animals in the forest to come there and seek refuge. She works hard to make sure that everything is in the correct order that it should be. She is my other half," said the sage.

"Will you be joining me at the ashram with Shakti, oh great sage?" asked Nivritti.

The sage let out a large belly laugh and his face wrinkled. "No, no, Nivritti, I cannot join Shakti, for if I do, the two of us and the ashram would disappear," and he continued to laugh. Again the light shone from his face and his body seemed to be made of light. The bluish hue also hung around the sage.

Nivritti was unsure what the sage meant but he continued through the forest for another half mile. The silence had been overrun now by a cacophony of animal sounds, and the undergrowth and brush were noticeably lighter. He could hear the birds chirping loudly in the background. The noises of the forest and animals seemed to come together in some sort of harmony. He had not heard it like this before, it was like a melodious symphony of nature.

After a few minutes he could clearly see the ashram.

The ashram was a clay building the size of a large house. It was surrounded by all manner of plants, shrubs and flowers. Animals too were present, numerous deer walking calmly in the front of the ashram where there was a small grassy area. He spotted a large black-and-white patched cow standing next to the well. It was not tied or harnessed. He could see behind the house the edge of a large pond or lake with ducks and white swans swimming gracefully.

The house was raised and had an open clay atrium, like a forecourt. A middle-aged lady clad in a saffron sari was busily brushing using a duster like the one the ladies in Gondyala used to clean their houses. She looked up at him as if startled. "Ahh, Nivritti, come in, come in!" she gushed.

As he came closer he noticed that she was a woman of maybe fifty with several clear wrinkle lines and a few grey streaks adorning her hair. She had that same appearance of light about her that Lord Shiva had. It was as if she was not solid matter and if Nivritti had reached out to touch her, his hand would have passed straight through. He could make out the bluish haze around her also. They were obviously made of the same stuff, he concluded.

"I am Shakti, welcome to my house," she said as she turned and gestured for him to follow her in. Her movements were brisk yet graceful, as if tranquility in motion.

Once in the ashram she offered him a mango and some water. The cut mango had a lustrous dark yellow color and was juicy and sweet. It was ripe to perfection.

"I met your husband, Lord Shiva," explained Nivritti.

"Yes, I know," said Shakti. "He is always around here in one form or other, though I can never seem to find him when there's any work to be done!" She smirked.

"He told me that you are seeking the truth."
"Yes, that is correct," said Nivritti. "I wish to know the nature of god."
"That is a lofty goal. I'm sure if you look hard enough you'll be able to find it," she said.
"Would you like to see our lake?" she continued, as if changing the subject.
"Oh, oh, I would love to," replied Nivritti, caught off guard by the sudden offer.
The lake was calm and still, the water flat, no ripples, just a dark bluish-grey color reflecting the dense brush around and the sky above. It was about one hundred yards across and Nivritti wondered whether it was a natural lake in the jungle or had somehow been conjured into existence by the mystical couple. "Have a look in the water," offered Shakti as she waved her hand across the water. Nivritti gazed at his own reflection and felt his head becoming lighter. He felt as he was somehow being pulled into the water. He tried to resist but it was futile. He was terrified. He felt himself being sucked under the water and was surrounded by bubbles and reeds. He saw a small shoal of fish and again felt himself being drawn deeper under the water.

His fear vanished. The lake opened up below into a vast deep ocean and in it he saw millions of fish of all kinds swimming in harmony, darting this way and that. He saw huge sea animals such as sharks and whales that he had seen only in books or films. He was sucked deeper, and now creatures appeared that he had never seen before, huge reptiles and scaled creatures that dwarfed the whales he had seen, with fins and tails the size of a ship's sails. Deeper and deeper until there were no more creatures, just the vast blue ocean.

"Huhh," he muttered. In an instant he was back in his body. He felt himself. He was dry. Had he just dreamed that experience? He was still leaning over the water gazing at a reflection of himself. He turned his head to Shakti.

"Having fun, are we?" she smiled. "Take a look at your reflection in the water."

"What do you see?" she asked

Nivritti looked into the still water. In the water he could make out his dark brown skin and his brown eyes. He could see his black hair swept back over his head, covering his ears.

He was not sure what Shakti meant. Was this some sort of test?

"I see a reflection of myself," he said.

"Very good," exclaimed Shakti, as if he had made some startling discovery.

"You the subject, are seeing your reflection... which is the object."

"Now tell me what you see," she said as she leaned her head over the water.

To his amazement there was no reflection of Shakti in the water. It was as if she was invisible. He gazed at her lightness. Perhaps she was not solid matter, after all. Why would her reflection not appear?

"If there is no object, then there can be no reflection," she said as if trying to coax him to some realization. His mind was confused She leaned back.

"I don't know what I just saw, oh great Shakti. I do not understand," said Nivritti. He felt that perhaps he was not smart enough to grasp this spiritual knowledge.

"Intellectual knowledge is the same as ignorance in this place, Nivritti," she exclaimed as if answering his thought.

"Nivritti, Shiva and I are one. There only ever has been, and will always be, only one. All things you see manifest around you in the world, including yourself, are all still part of the one. The subject and the object are the same. To enjoy my manifested ashram I have to separate from Lord Shiva. I have to create an object that appears separate from the subject. We are like night and day. Yet in the realm of the sun, night and day has no meaning. It is merely an arbitrary distinction."

Nivritti struggled to grasp the concept. The words had meaning but he did not understand.

Shakti continued. "If I alone exist, how can I enjoy the manifestation? It exists so that you can enjoy the play of divine consciousness. The duality you perceive, with you as the doer or the seeker separate from the rest of the creation, is false.

Just as you awoke this morning from your deep sleep and are now here, so also Shiva wakes from the unmanifest state and creation appears. So similarly when he sleeps the creation is absorbed back into him. This process is like a circle where all points represent both creation and absorption. There is no beginning and no end, there just is."

She paused, seeing Nivritti's dilemma.

"The tongue cannot taste itself," she said with a wry smile.

Nivritti was not sure what he had heard, but knew that hearing the words and understanding them was part of the path that lay ahead of him. It was appearing more difficult than he had imagined.

That evening Nivritti enjoyed a delicious meal of dal and rice cooked by Shakti's divine hand. The flavor of the dal seemed just perfect, neither too strong and overwhelming nor too bland.

Shakti talked about the ashram and the animals and how she kept everything in order. Nivritti listened in silence but had an overwhelming feeling of calm and satisfaction. It was not that he didn't wish to talk as well, it was just that he had nothing to say. His silence was perfect.

The following morning he packed his clothes and supplies of food and water from the ashram. Shakti came to him and asked if he would like to look at her cow. He had seen it when he had first arrived at the ashram, it was a large black and white beast that he noticed was not tethered.

"This is Kamadhenu, our wish-fulfilling cow," said Shakti. "She will grant you one desire that will be fulfilled. Anything you want, Nivritti, money, wealth, fame, you name it."

Nivritti gazed at the cow and his mind started to fill with fanciful ideas. What if he was rich beyond his dreams? He could have the largest house in the village, maybe even own his own car, a large white ambassador like the one Santosh owned. But as he started to think he realized that even if he had all these things, the sense of loss and sorrow he felt because of his mother would not go away. He would still not be able to find peace. He would not be happy.

"Oh great Kamadhenu, I wish to know the Truth, I want to be enlightened," he exclaimed. A feeling of relief and pride overcame him as he spoke. He was going to find the Truth.

The cow gazed at him, seemingly unaffected by his profound utterance. He was unsure if his wish would be manifest or not.

Later that day he took leave of Shakti and continued his journey through the forest. His thoughts dwelled on why, despite having met Lord Shiva and his consort, Shakti, he was unable to get the answers to what he sought. Why was god himself unable to show him the truth and make him enlightened? What more would it take?

Lord Gahininath- The Guru

Nivritti continued wandering for several more hours through the forest. It was not quite as dense as before and the undergrowth seemed to open as if a natural path had been created. He felt the humidity rising and gazing up through the dense canopy he could see dark storm clouds gathering. He started picking up his pace with a sense of urgency. He would need to find some sort of shelter before the storm arrived. Ahead, he could make out a structure and as he approached he saw that it was an ancient temple. He could make out the crumbling bricks, peeping out through the vegetation and vines that adorned the walls. The edge of the temple had partially collapsed, leaving a large corner entrance that was overgrown with shrubs. He cut his way through and entered the temple. The roof had long since collapsed, as had several of the walls. The stone floor was also in a poor state, worn down by time and the elements. Nivritti could make out the altar at the far end of the temple, about fifty feet away. No doubt his ancestors must have worshipped here with their rituals and rites. The temple had a musty odor similar to that in old libraries, the smell of damp and mold.

In the center of the temple in front of the altar were two giant carved stone feet. The toes were facing him and the sculpture appeared to be in near perfect shape. No moss had overgrown the feet and the carving did not seem to have aged. At the tip of the right big toe was a small hemispheric indentation. Nivritti rubbed his finger into it. It was smooth, as if made purposefully by the original artisans or possibly by the friction of thousands of people's hands touching this spot. He gazed at the feet for a few minutes. Why had the ancients placed the feet of the lord as the main object of their worship? He was perplexed. Surely a great sculpture of the Lord Vishnu or Shiva would have been more appropriate. Why the feet, and what was the significance of the right big toe?

He sat against one of the crumbling walls and pondered. This journey was creating more questions than answers. As he sat there he could feel the raindrops start to land on his face, at first gently, but then harder and harder. The noise of the water in the temple started to create a loud drumming noise. He would have to find shelter. He gathered his possessions and placed his cotton pack over his head to fend off the rain. As he exited the temple the hairs on his neck stood up and he was gripped by a feeling of unease as if he was being watched. He gazed around through the screen of rain that was lashing him, but he could see nothing.

He began to trudge through the mud, each step growing harder and harder as the mud and water weighed down his feet. He was now walking looking at the ground a few feet ahead of him so he didn't slip and fall. He glanced up and saw a flash of movement through the brush. Nivritti was suddenly overcome by an intense fear. He recognized the shape that he had fleetingly glimpsed. The jungle was known to harbor tigers, and he had heard stories his whole life of some poor villager or other meeting an untimely and savage end after an encounter with one of the creatures. There was usually not much left of the poor soul – if they were even found at all. His mind began to race with fear. What if he met the same fate? No one would ever know. He started to run, pushing the leaves and brush aside, blind terror his only guide. He looked back and made out the shape again. It was following him. He saw what looked like a narrow path ascending a small hillock and ran faster. There was less brush here and he rose slowly up through the canopy. Was the great beast still in pursuit? he wondered, still gripped by his terror. Halfway up the hill he noticed a small cave and instinctively decided to go in. He would stand a better chance here than if he were attacked from behind. He stopped in the entrance out of the rain and gazed back. He could see nothing except the rain, which had created a haze of mist and vapor. He waited a few minutes but nothing came, and gradually his terror subsided.

The noise of the raindrops gradually faded and left only the mist. As Nivritti gazed over the jungle he took in a deep breath. It was as if the mist and air had somehow concentrated all the elements of the jungle, and as he breathed deeply in and out he could feel it permeating his lungs and being.

He turned around and looked into the cave. He could see about thirty feet inside. It was about ten feet high, with damp muddy walls. He was unsure if it was a natural cave or had somehow been carved out, perhaps as a rest stop for travelers through the jungle. He walked into the darkness. Ahead he could make out the faint flicker of a fire. His fear had gone now as he walked ahead towards the light.

The light was indeed a small fire, its flames dancing and illuminating a yogi seated in deep meditation. The yogi appeared to be in a deep trance. Nivritti could not make out his features well in the dim light, but he appeared to be seated on a deerskin rug. Lying on the floor next to him was a small earthen water pot and a yoga-danda.

Without any prompting the yogi opened his eyes.

"Nivritti. I've been waiting a long time for you."

"Who are you, oh great yogi?" asked Nivritti. He was not surprised that the yogi knew his name. He knew that nothing on this journey was by chance.

"I am Lord Gahininath," said the yogi. "I am your Guru. I have been waiting here for your arrival so that I can initiate you in the nature of true knowledge."

Nivritti's heart started pounding with excitement. Perhaps this was the person who would reveal the truth to him and lead him to enlightenment.

"I am ready, oh great sage," Nivritti said, wanting to confirm the old man's inference.

The old sage continued, "What do you know of the truth from the scriptures and shastras you have read?"

Nivritti looked down sheepishly. "I am afraid that I have not read any of the great works, nor have I truly contemplated or meditated on the nature of truth."

The sage sat silently gazing past Nivritti as if he was barely visible. Perhaps he would not think him a worthy student to receive this knowledge, worried Nivritti.

"Then you are the perfect student for me," exclaimed the sage. "Come, sit across from me and I will show you what you need to know."

Nivritti hurriedly sat down across from the old man, eager and excited for what he hoped would follow.

At last he would know the truth! The old man started to explain. "Before the phenomenal world around you was ever created, before the sun and stars and moon ever existed, even before time and space itself, there was Lord Shiva. But of course you met him, did you not?" he said as a wry smile came over his face. He continued. "Imagine a large blank canvas. That is Lord Shiva. Existing by himself, no space, no time, no creation. The potential for all that is still yet to be manifest but is yet unmanifest exists on the blank canvas. In the realm of the canvas there is no space or time, no manifestation. Shiva exists with the perception of 'I.' There is no 'I am,' just 'I,' no other. In the canvas there is no duality. "Shiva sets in motion a painting on part of the canvas—creation, if you will. The painting is considered the manifestation and is looked after by Shiva's consort Shakti. Now, they are one and the same, but one is the dynamic aspect of creation, the painting, and the other is the static aspect, the canvas. Two sides of the same coin. Since everything on the canvas, including the paint, is ultimately Shiva, there is still only 'I.' In order to enjoy the ever-changing painting Shiva has to create a false duality. That way, the beings in the creation can enjoy the work. The created duality is by its very nature an essential component of the creation, but is also at its core a false duality. You are living in the creation or painting and experience that very same duality. You feel you are an individual being, separate from the world around you. That is not so. The nature of the canvas is divine consciousness. Underlying the whole of this creation is the canvas of divine consciousness onto which it is painted. Everything around you, including you, is made of the same consciousness. "You are made in the image of the Lord." The sage continued, as Nivritti listened, transfixed. "Within you exists the Shiva and the Shakti. The Shiva exists in the crown region of your head and the Shakti exists at the base of your spine. They are artificially kept separate in you so that you experience the duality of creation. If they unite you will experience a non-dual state where there is only the 'I.' At that point you will perceive the whole of creation as a manifestation of yourself. That state is the state that you seek, the state of enlightenment." Nivritti sat silently. He implicitly knew the sage's words were the truth. "At the base of your spine lies the dormant Shakti, or Kundalini. We describe it as coiled serpent because that is how she appears with her golden luster. There are seven points along your spine that prevent the Kundalini from rising and maintain the illusion of the creation as a duality. The lower three are where most people experience their consciousness. Once the Kundalini reaches the middle chakra in the region of the heart, termed the anhaat chakra, then the individual starts to experience transcendent states. Anhaat means 'unstruck' and indicates that the individual will begin perceiving vibrations from the canvas that underlies creation. The vibrations are sounds and energy that have yet to appear in the painting portion of creation but which exist in an as-yet unmanifest state in the canvas. They are unmanifest sound and described as unstruck as they are not created by anything."

Nivritti interjected triumphantly, "So by meditation and reading of the scriptures, and of course by leading a righteous life, one can cause the Kundalini to rise and experience enlightenment?"

Gahnininath gazed at him in silence.

"No" he replied. "Those activities are useful, like creating the right soil and tilling the land in preparation for growing the rice. But for rice to grow the seed must first be planted.

"One could read all the scriptures in the world and meditate for a thousand years and still not perceive the truth.

"For the Kundalini to rise requires the infusion of divine energy. This is called Shaktipat and has to be given by an enlightened guru. A person that walks in the Light.

"Until then, all the efforts of the student will be futile.

"This is an intrinsic principle of the creation. The guru should not be viewed as a person but as a cosmic truth, a safeguard in the creation allowing the seeker of truth to know his essential divine nature.

"I have waited here for you, Nivritti, knowing the time would come when you would be ready to receive this rare gift. When the student is ready and has made effort on the path of enlightenment, the guru will always appear."

Nivritti, sitting cross legged, leaned in and listened intently to the old sage. He felt his mind become silent and content. No thoughts ran through it. He knew in his heart the truth of the sage's words. "Sit up with your back straight and place the tip of your index finger to the tip of your thumb, palm open, facing upwards. Place your hands on your thigh close to your knees," instructed the sage. "Now, I want you to imagine your breath starting at the level of your heart. As you breathe in count the in breath up to the level of your forehead. As you breathe in you are going to mentally count one, one, one. At the level of the forehead is the Ajna chakra. Here you will suspend your breath and in your mind count two, two, two. As you exhale back down to the heart chakra you will count three, three, three. Once there you will suspend your exhaled breath and count four, four, four. Mentally restart the next breath by reciting zero and then start the cycle of inspiration again."

Nivritti began to do as the sage instructed, slowly counting his breath in, suspending, and exhaling.

He kept wondering if he was doing it right. After a few minutes the sage instructed him further. "Now drop it to a two count. Inhale with one, one, suspend with two, two and so on."

Nivritti continued, and as he did so he felt his mind gradually quieting down, focusing intently on the numbers and the breath.

Several minutes passed and the sage said, "Now go to a one count, inspiration one, suspension two, exhalation three, and suspension four."

Nivritti complied. His mind became even quieter, and he noticed his breath become more subtle.

"Now I want you to stop reciting two at the suspension point in the Ajna chakra and just keep it silent," said the sage.

Several more minutes passed. Nivritti was now counting one, then silence at the Ajna chakra, three for exhalation and four in the suspension. He noticed that the period of silence was getting longer. He tried to hold it for as long as was comfortable. He realized that his need to take in a breath had diminished considerably and the suspension point in the Ajna chakra grew longer and longer.

He started to perceive a strange sensation. It was a buzzing sensation, almost like something was vibrating. It was coming from his Ajna chakra. He could also perceive a small and indistinct light that was intermittently appearing in the center of his vision.

He realized he was no longer aware of his bodily senses, he could not feel his hands or fingers. He made out the sage rising and felt him place his hand gently on top of his head.

The light suddenly started to get brighter and brighter as if he was gazing at the sun. It began to fill the whole of his internal vision. He noticed an intense pressure in his forehead and a feeling of lightness. Slowly the lightness became more intense and he felt himself drawn into the light. It was uncontrollable.

Nivritti could clearly see himself now. He was several feet above his own body and could see the old sage standing over him, hand still on his forehead. He was softly reciting some mantras. As he gazed at himself it was as if he was gazing at someone else. His feeling of "I"-ness for Nivritti had gone. As he gazed around he could make out the cave, but the walls seemed to have bright, almost incandescent glow to them. He took himself higher out of the cave, effortlessly moving through the walls as if they were nonexistent, and gazed across the jungle.

It was nighttime now and he could hear the night symphony of the jungle. It seemed as if it was part of him. As he looked up he could see the moon and the stars in the night sky. They seemed brighter and luminescent. Again he had the feeling that they were part of him. He effortlessly moved around but could make out a fine chord of light that appeared to still be connecting him to his body. It did not seem to impede his movement at all. He had not previously perceived the world as such. After a few minutes he decided to return to his body, and brought himself back to the cave. In an instant he was back within himself, engulfed in the brilliant white light. He no longer had the perception of "I am Nivritti," all the problems and anxieties of that person had no relevance to him. In the light he found a feeling of contentment. It was not happiness, per se, but deeper. It was a completeness that he had never had. There was no desire, no feeling that it could end. It was true bliss.

It was a non-relational state of completeness and being. It was his natural state, his essential nature.

Time did not exist here.

With a start Nivritti suddenly found himself back to his worldly state, still sitting in lotus pose, or padmasan. The light was gone. He opened his eyes. The sage sat across from him and was rocking slowly two and fro reciting mantras. His eyes were closed. The mantras had a musical quality to them and the sage appeared to be engrossed in them. He was unsure how long he had been in the light. The cave appeared as it had before, dark mud walls, the glow gone. After a few minutes the sage opened his eyes and gazed at Nivritti. "There, it is done," he exclaimed. "How did you enjoy the Shaktipat?" he said with a smile

Nivritti was lost for words. He had just had the most intense experience of his life and felt at a loss. "Incredible," he said. "Just incredible. "Thank you, oh great sage. I am truly blessed to have had this experience." It was beyond words. Nivritti spent the night in the cave, and the following morning helped gather some wood for the old sage's fire. As he gazed at the old man he felt a kinship with him, a love almost greater than the love he had for his mother. He had barely met this man and yet the feeling was intense. He did not know where it came from but as he bid the old sage farewell he felt his stomach tighten as if a large stone had been dropped into it. The parting gave him a feeling of sadness, as if just being in the sage's presence was joy itself.

The sage waved Nivritti off and turned back into the cave, muttering to himself, "Shivo Ham, Shivo Ham…" just softly enough to be out of earshot of Nivritti.

Vani Guru

Nivritti continued on his journey. The storm had passed and travelling through the forest now seemed easier. He felt a new awareness, a confidence that he was going to find what he was seeking. He knew he was fortunate to have met his guru. He knew that this was an auspicious event in any seeker's life.

The forest cleared and he came to a ridge overlooking a small valley. He could make out a small farm house and several pastures with cows and bullocks grazing. He could see the neat rows of the water filling rice paddies. He headed down the ridge in the direction of the farm.

As he approached he came upon an old banyan tree. He saw a large branch on which were perched three crows. They were squawking as they hopped back and forth, pecking at some berries that were hanging from the branch. He stopped and gazed at them. They continued their activity oblivious to him. On a branch higher up he noticed another crow. It was silently gazing at the other three. It stood motionless. He watched for a few minutes and then continued his walk. He had now descended into the valley and was walking along a small muddy path to the farmhouse. The sun was beaming through as the rainclouds slowly dissipated.

He walked past a small earthen well and towards the farmhouse. It was the same general design as other earthen houses in his village. It had a raised clay courtyard at the front and a veranda. A wooden swing was gently rocking in the soft breeze. There was a large Om symbol painted on the front wall of the house just above the front door. It was saffron and barely visible against the light brown clay wall.

"Hello," he called out, hoping not to startle anyone. There was no answer. He could hear a noise coming from behind the house in the paddy field. He walked round the house and saw a man with a hoe shoring up one of the rice paddy lines. His feet were immersed in the water. He was a slender man wearing a white dhoti and across his bare chest was a zanva, a white thread consisting of three intertwining strands that symbolized that he was a Brahmin. "Hello," said Nivritti, this time louder so the Brahmin would hear him. The man looked up and smiled. He put down the hoe and came towards Nivritti. As he approached, Nivritti could see his face. He had a dark brown complexion, having obviously spent a good portion of his time out in the sun, yet his skin was smooth and unwrinkled. Nivritti estimated he must be in his forties. He had a jet black moustache which appeared perfectly manicured.

"Hello, I am Nivritti. I am making a pilgrimage through the jungle in order to meet the seven sages," said Nivritti, not quite knowing why he used the word pilgrimage. "Ah, yes, well, welcome to my humble abode," said the man. "My name is Vani, and some people call me Vani guru. "My name, Vani, means 'speech,' and I believe I can help you on your journey," he said. "Let us go inside." Later that afternoon, Vani guru and Nivritti were seated cross legged across from each other on the veranda. The overhanging Om symbol observed them silently. Vani turned his head to the symbol and slowly gazed back at Nivritti. "The Om symbolizes the planes of consciousness in which one exists," said the Brahmin. He continued, "The triadic shape represents the waking, dreaming, and deep sleep states that make up one's worldly life. From the moment you are born you live your life in that triad. In the worldly state you associate 'I' with your mind, body, or intellect. The senses are turned outward. In the dream state the 'I' is the dreamer and the association with the body and mind is less. In this state the senses are turned inward. In the deep sleep state, there is no association of the mind or body so there is no 'knowledge' of the state. The states are separate from each other. The deep sleep state transcends into the dream state and that transcends into the waking state. The individual believes he is then 'awake' and in his natural state.

He is not.

"The line above the Om sign and the point above it represent the state of Turiya. This is the underlying foundational consciousness over which these other states are laid. One can experience this state briefly in the transition from the dreaming state to the waking state and vice versa, if the yogi pays attention.

"It is also to be found in the space between one thought and the subsequent thought. In the Turiya state one perceives oneself and the world as a manifestation of divine consciousness.

"In Turiya, one's experience is that of the ear of the ear, the eye of the eye, and the mind of the mind. It is a transcendent state where the knower, the knowledge, and the known are one, where duality ceases."

"Is that the highest state of enlightenment?" interjected Nivritti.

"No," replied the Brahmin, "but it is close."

"How does one attain such a state?" asked Nivritti.

"One can attain Turiya by different means. Deep meditation allows the yogi to maintain a constant awareness of the underlying Pure consciousness," answered the Brahmin.

"Remembrance of the guru is the best means. One must dissolve the ego, thoughts, and desires by keeping the guru in one's heart.

"That is the means not only of obtaining Turiya but also of transcending it," said the Brahmin. He smiled as he looked at Nivritti. "This is not an intellectual field. The truth can never be grasped by intellect. It dwells beyond the world of opposites. It can only be 'known' by experience.

"Come, let us sit and meditate together." He gestured Nivritti towards some cushions lying at the side of the veranda.

Within a few minutes the two men were seated in padmasan with their buttocks on the cushions and feet resting on the floor.

"Before any meditation one must salute the Sad-guru, the guru who dwells within us. Then you must salute your own guru, Lord Gahininath, and place his feet upon your head," said Vani guru.

Nivritti sat in padmasan with his fingers wrapped around his thumbs as instructed by the Brahmin. He closed his eyes and in his mind placed his guru's feet on top of his head and ran through the salutations

"Sad-gurunath maharaj Ki-jai, Gahininath-guru maharaj Ki-jai, Vani-guru maharaj Ki-jai."

As he completed his internal prayer he felt the vibration he had felt in the cave. It started subtly in his forehead and became more intense. He noticed that the vibration created an excitement in him that distracted him and thereby diminished the intensity of the vibration. He tried to stay relaxed and concentrated on the mantra given him by the Brahmin.

"Guru-om, guru-om, guru-om."

As he recited he noticed thoughts about Santosh, Janesh, and his mother arising. He continued to internally chant. On and on he continued. He noticed that his breath had slowed as in the cave. He could no longer feel his physical body. The vibration was now in his forehead. It seemed to move or change tone slightly. For a few minutes he felt a high pitched tone emanating from his left ear, almost like an invisible beam of sound and vibration was being emitted from him. The chanting continued.

He perceived his breath gradually subsiding until he was not breathing at all. The extraneous thoughts had all gone. His mind was completely silent save for the vibrations that continued. The internal mantra also stopped. There was just silence, no thoughts, no breath.

He felt a sudden "drop" from where he was to a state of total silence and stillness. He perceived now a sense of "I"-ness, but with no association to Nivritti. As he bathed in this state he felt a rising sensation of bliss that kept increasing in intensity. The "I" that he was in was consumed by the bliss. In the "I"-ness was no desire, no pain, no suffering. It was a state free from any of the dualities of his waking life. He could have stayed in that state for eternity, for he was free from the constraints of time. There was nothing that could be added or taken away from that state. It was complete in itself. He did not want it to end.

"Open your eyes," instructed the Brahmin.

Nivritti reluctantly obeyed him.

He opened his eyes and gazed around. His mind was still and the feeling of bliss still permeated his being.

"Ananda means bliss," said the Brahmin. "That is what you experienced and are now experiencing. It is part of your true nature, your divine nature."

Nivritti listened, his mind still silent, submerged in the bliss.

"From now on when you meditate you must try and get to a state of bliss. You must transcend the three planes of consciousness and try and experience the Turiya state," said the Brahmin.

"There can be no token meditation, no ticking it off like some task to be completed. Only by constant diligent effort can the seeker hope to attain true realization of the Self."

Nivritti listened to the Brahmin's words and understood them at a deeper level. He was still immersed in the bliss, but was able to converse with the Brahmin. Thoughts of what to say seemed to arise spontaneously. He felt as if he had made a small leap in his understanding. The leap was not an intellectual leap but more of a spiritual step-up.

That evening he ate with the Brahmin. They had rice and a curd made from a sour plant and concocted into a dark brownish liquid that they poured over the rice. It was tasty, with a somewhat tart sensation on the tongue which contrasted nicely with the blandness of the rice. Pithi and rice, what the poorest villagers ate. Nivritti gratefully ate the pithi and rice and couldn't help but notice that he was eating a pauper's meal in the house of one of the richest men he had ever met. The following morning Nivritti helped the Brahmin shore up some of the rows of the paddy field. The cool water on his feet contrasted with the gradually warming morning sun. He enjoyed the work, as it gave him a feeling of being connected to the earth. He would not ordinarily have done this kind of manual labor at home. Usually farm labor was done by the poorest of the poor.

They continued for several hours as the sun continued its ascent. Finally the Brahmin gestured towards the shade of the trees and they headed over with a small clay water pot. As Nivritti poured the cool water in his mouth he felt his energy return. The cool shade was a relief. The two men sat silently gazing over their work. "Why are you called Vani?" asked Nivritti, breaking the silence. "Speech and sound itself are very important in the creation," said the Brahmin. He continued. "At the beginning of creation it is sound that initiates the formation of space. It is sound and vibration that links the manifest universe with the un-manifest universe. It is sound and vibration underlying this creation you see before you. It is sound and words that allow you to ascend the arc of evolution back to Shiva." "The words you utter at a verbal level are at the final stage of a journey that began in the un-manifest universe. When you talk of an object at the Vaikhari level, which is the level of speech, there is a definite distinction between the sound and the object. There is a duality. They are separate. At the level of Shiva in the un-manifest state there is no differentiation between the sound and the object itself. There is not even a potentiality for differentiation at this level. There is no duality between the two and it is at what is termed the Para level. Once there appears a potentiality for differentiation, this is termed the Pasyanti level.

The two are still one but the potential for duality exists. At the Madhyama level the distinction between the two has arisen at the thought level in the mind but the duality is not totally expressed."

The Brahmin sat silently gazing at Nivritti. He sensed his confusion.

Nivritti could not understand what the Brahmin was telling him. He understood the words but their true meaning was indiscernible.

"Nivritti, when the yogi meditates on a mantra such as we did with Guru-Om, he contemplates it at these different levels. If he speaks it out loud then it is at the Vaikhari level. If it is recited at the level of thought then it is at the Madhyama level. With constant repetition the yogi's understanding of it reaches the Pasyanti level and eventually the Para level. The silence between the Guru-Om is where the yogi is at the Para level. Each recitation of the mantra manifests from the silence and descends in an arc to the Vaikhari level," said Vani.

"Nivritti, when the yogi experiences anything or says anything, he is the subject. He speaks or sees or experiences an object. He is always aware that the consciousness that is the underlying witness of himself is none other than that which is the underlying consciousness of the object itself," said the Brahmin.

They sat in silence for a few minutes.

"Akhanda mandalakaram!" exclaimed the Brahmin.

"What does that mean?" asked Nivritti.

"It is a mahavakhya, or great words," said Vani. "Divine consciousness is like a circle with an infinite circumference and a center everywhere. These mahavakhyas are to be contemplated in meditation and not to be intellectually reasoned out. As your meditation becomes deeper you will obtain spiritual knowledge that will come to you in the silence. This is true knowledge, or Jnana."

The Brahmin could see the dejection on Nivritti's face lift a little.

"Nivritti, you are expending great effort on this path, and that is what is required initially to progress," he said.

Later that day the Brahmin explained how the debt to the four levels of speech and the four planes of consciousness would need to be transcended to attain a state of total enlightenment.

Nivritti felt better in the knowledge that he was on the right path and that spiritual knowledge was not something that could be read or taught with words. He truly understood now, for the first time, that direct experience of it was all that was important.

The sun does not need any other light to illuminate itself, for it is self-effulgent.

Jnana- Pure Knowledge

It had been several days since Nivritti had left Vani guru. He had continued his journey through the forest. He had begun a daily practice of meditation, beginning, as instructed by the Brahmin, with the salutations to his gurus. The meditation had increased in intensity and he would feel the vibration of the Kundalini in his head as he began. The length of the meditations had also increased, as he would sit until his mind had reached a state of total silence. He noticed that each time the experience was slightly different: sometimes the vibration would predominate and other times an intense white light would appear. He no longer doubted that he was doing it correctly. He knew the truth of his experience.

He had stopped in a small grove of mango trees and sat down under one of them for some shade. It was late afternoon and the sun's heat made the shade necessary.

As he sat there a subtle vibration began in his left ear and grew more intense. He sat observing the grove. The vibration continued and its tone changed to a high pitch. He knew this was not coming from his physical body. It was calling to him.

He crossed his legs and adopted his meditation pose.

His breath stilled as he contemplated the Guru-om mantra. Shallower and shallower his breath became until it was almost imperceptible. And then it stopped.

Sitting in his extra-temporal inner silence, Nivritti began to notice the presence of a being. It appeared in his inner vision. It was a sage dressed in saffron robes with an intense white light permeating around him. Beyond the light there extended various layers of intense bright colors which created a rainbow-like aura around the sage.

"I am Jnana," said the being. It spoke no words, but Nivritti could hear the voice appear in his inner consciousness.

"I am pure knowledge and am here to explain my nature to you so you will understand." Nivritti's mind remained still, his breath imperceptible.

Jnana guru continued, "You seek knowledge, which is the opposite of ignorance. Yet you understand that anything in the world of opposites is not the truth. Joy and sorrow, good and bad, life and death, all exist only in the world of duality. The same is true for knowledge and ignorance.

"The knowledge you are acquiring is burning the ignorance you have within you, yet will only lead to another state of ignorance."

"What then is needed, Oh Jnana-guru?" enquired Nivritti.

Jnana-guru gestured for Nivritti to look down in front of himself. There he could see a lamp containing a ball of white camphor, which was burning with a small flame. The flame burned for several minutes as the camphor became smaller and smaller, until it was at its end. Suddenly the flame grew very bright and in an instant it was gone. The camphor and the flame had both extinguished each other. "The knowledge you are acquiring is like the flame burning the camphor of ignorance, but once your knowledge reaches its zenith it, too, will cease to exist along with the ignorance." In his stillness Nivritti sensed the sage's teaching but did not grasp it fully. Before him suddenly appeared a chair bathed in bright sunlight. Nivritti gazed at it and could almost feel the heat of the intense sunlight. Then there was darkness and the chair could no longer be seen. "I see the chair in the light of the sun, in the light of knowledge, and in the darkness of ignorance the chair is not seen," thought Nivritti. "No," said Jnana guru. "In your ignorance, or darkness, you see no chair. In the light of relative knowledge, you see the chair. Yet the sunlight itself is not seen. You see a reflection of the sunlight from the chair. The two are distinct. The visible chair is the relative knowledge you possess, it is reflected Pure consciousness like the reflected sunlight. The sun of Pure consciousness itself is unaffected, whether the chair is bathed in its light or not."

Nivritti gazed up at the sage. The sage was gone and in his inner vision he could now see the shadow of the moon. It appeared as a full moon. As he watched he could see a crescent of darkness appear across it, getting bigger and bigger until the moon was covered in the darkness.

"The moon is seen in the light of relative knowledge and in the darkness of ignorance appears to disappear. Yet the moon itself is affected by neither the light nor the darkness and continues to exist," said the sage. "The moon is Pure knowledge or consciousness and the light and dark exist in the realm of relative knowledge and ignorance, in the false world of duality."

Nivritti sat motionless. In his inner silence, his lesson continued.

The sage appeared before Nivritti. He was standing sideways before him and gazing into a large mirror. Nivritti could see the sage's reflection.

"I am Pure consciousness," said the sage. "In the mirror I see my reflection. There is a duality created by the mirror. The subject and the object are the same. There is only the process of seeing.

"There is no difference between the seer, the seen, and the seeing. That is Jnana or Pure knowledge. That is true meditation."

Nivritti felt himself lean forward in his mind and gaze at the sage's reflection in the mirror. The sage and his reflection seemed to extend into infinity, with endless visions of the sage and his reflections—the Pure consciousness and its reflection basking in each other's glory with no beginning or end.

Nivritti intuitively knew that this was the key to perceiving the truth.

"What are the methods by which this view of the world can be attained?" asked Nivritti.

"You have reached this state by meditating on the Guru-om mantra. You have done well and advanced far into the spiritual realm in a short time. When you sit again for meditation on this mantra your attention should be focused on the gap between the guru-oms. As you recite lengthen the gap and keep your mind still. In the gap is neither knowledge nor ignorance but the Pure consciousness. No effort must be made to try and perceive or understand it. It cannot be understood or quantified. It is beyond knowledge and ignorance. It is beyond the known and the unknown. You must just be. Effortless effort is what is required."

The sage paused. As he "spoke," Nivritti could see the white aura around him intensify.

"Another method is to drop all associations of the mind and keep it focused on the present moment. The past and future do not exist and neither does time in the world of Pure consciousness. There is only the infinite now. If one is able to do this, one stills all the fluctuations of the mind and resides in the immediateness of the Pure consciousness.

"The third way has been shown to you by Vani-guru. By viewing everything around you as the center of a circle of Pure consciousness with infinite circumference, one can perceive the state of Pure knowledge.

"The fourth way is in the transition from the dream sleep state to the awake state, where the yogi has not yet associated himself with his 'I am body' state. If care is taken the yogi can experience the underlying Pure consciousness in this transit point.

"This Jnana cannot be objectified, nor revealed by words. It is beyond the four levels of speech and the four planes of consciousness. It is neither known nor unknown, it is neither existent nor non-existent, it is neither present nor absent. In it there is no 'knowingness.'

"It is revealed in the absence of Absolute silence."

So saying, the sage faded from Nivritti's inner view. He was back in the silence of his meditation.

Sat, Chit, and Ananda- the Trio

Nivritti completed his meditation and continued walking through the mango grove. He could see a few small huts at the edge of the grove and could make out some villagers standing on the porch of one of the houses. As he approached he could make out a small clay hut with a rickety wooden porch. A small dirt path ran past it and he could see several houses further along it.

On the porch of the first house there stood three identical triplets. They were dressed in white dhotis and each was wearing a white zanva that ran diagonally across one shoulder. He estimated they were in their early twenties, certainly not more than a few years older than himself. All three had clean-shaven heads and smooth olive skin. It was evident that they were not farm laborers.

Nivritti approached the porch and stood in front of the trio.

"Hello, Nivritti," said the first youth. "I am Sat, or existence, and these are my brothers Chit, or consciousness, and Ananda, or bliss. Our mother is Atman."

Nivritti knew that these three represented the term that ancient yogis and sages had used to describe the divine. Atman was the term used for the divinity within each individual.

Nivritti knew why they were here to greet him.

"We are described as three, but really we are the same. It is not possible to separate us," said Sat. "People often call us existence, consciousness, and bliss. In reality we are intertwined and inseparable. When we look at consciousness we see blissful existence and when we see existence we see conscious bliss. "I am the unmanifest state of my brothers. "Where there is the potentiality of manifestation then my brother Chit is predominant, and where the potentiality is manifest then Ananda is predominant. "Why don't you take a walk through our small hamlet and see the truth for yourself?" invited Sat, gesturing for Nivritti to go ahead along the path. Nivritti bowed his head slightly in acknowledgement and slowly started walking along the path. He gazed back at the three, but from this angle the three brothers appeared to be standing one behind the other, giving the appearance of one person. In the first hut he came upon an elderly man who was about to light a fire to cook some food. He could see the white soft camphor in the man's hands and smell its typical fragrance. The man lit the camphor and the fire started. The man picked up some seeds of wheat in his hand and looked up at Nivritti. Nivritti felt the vibration in his forehead and in his inner vision could see the flour and the cooked chapattis and the warm taste of the food on his tongue. Nivritti gazed at the man holding the seeds. The man smiled at him and continued his cooking. Nivritti continued to the next house. There, a young women in a sari was seated cross-legged. On her lap lay a veena, which she was busily restringing. She did not look up at Nivritti but was wholly engaged in her work, softly humming a melodious tune. As he watched her stringing the instrument, in his inner vision he could hear himself listening to the music and experiencing the tune. And then both the music and the listener were absorbed back into the silence. He stood gazing back at the veena. The young woman continued her stringing.

He turned and continued through the village. It was early afternoon and the sun was past its zenith. Ahead he saw a man looking at his shadow and marking the ground. He made a mark where his feet were and with a stick marked where the top of his head was on the shadow. When he changed position the length of his shadow would change and he would again mark it. Each shadow length was different, depending on where he was standing. Nivritti watched him for several minutes and then enquired, "What are you doing?"

The man looked at Nivritti and said, "I am measuring my height. I have figured out that since my shadow is a reflection of myself it should be a good way of measuring my height."

Nivritti smiled at the man's foolishness and continued to walk. He was nearing the end of the village and could see the where the path came to an end. Ahead was a wall of tall bamboo sugar cane about ten feet high which he could not see over. There was a farmer hunched over planting some sugar cane buds. Nivritti loved sugar cane juice and as he watched the farmer plant he could, in his mind's eye, see the sugar cane being wound through the sugar cane grinder and see the juice dripping into a glass. He could taste the delicious sweet nectar on his palate.

Nivritti stood watching the man planting the buds for several minutes. Then he looked around. The village was a cul-de-sac with no further path and so he turned around and headed back to the triplets.

When Nivritti returned to the trio, Sat asked him, "Now do you understand our nature, Nivritti? Do you have any questions?"

Nivritti paused. "On my journey so far I have intuitively understood the truth to be beyond the world of opposites, beyond the scope of words. Yet existence, consciousness, and bliss are three words and also have three opposites, non-existence, non-consciousness, and non-bliss."

He continued, "Why then have the sages used these words that exist in the world of opposites to describe the Truth?"

Sat smiled at Nivritti and said, "You have understood a lot, Nivritti. That is good. You will find many techniques that are rooted in the world of delusion that allow you to trace the path back to the ultimate. "The words Sat, Chit, and Ananda are not used to describe the Truth, as you correctly understand, but are used so that the yogi may contemplate their opposites. The yogi meditates on the Truth using the opposites and they cancel each other out. Therefore the existence and its absence, the consciousness and it absence, the joy and its absence are all negated. Once the delusion is destroyed and all the opposites are cancelled, what remains is the void or Shunya. The path for the three words comes to an end. Trying to return to the Truth by describing it as Sat, Chit, and Ananda is like the fool trying to measure his height by using his shadow.

"When your mind sees an object it views that object as being non-consciousness, while seeing itself as the consciousness. In reality, your mind is also the object and is also in the realm of non-consciousness. The underlying consciousness that is illuminating the mind, the mind of the mind if you will, is the Pure consciousness.

"The Pure existence, consciousness, and bliss are in the silence in which the potentiality for all things already exists. The music you heard from the veena already existed in the un-manifest state, as did the taste of the sugar cane juice. The listener of the music and the taster of the bread also existed in the un-manifest state.

"Similarly, the blissful state is not created, it is part of the underlying consciousness. It cannot be created nor experienced, it just is. It underlies your experiences when you are happy and also when you are sad."

Nivritti understood. He addressed the three. "Oh Satchitananda, please instruct me further in the how to find this state of void or Shunya."

"Remember, Nivritti, Shunya is described as void but is referred to as such due to the absence of all thought constructs, above time and space, where the knower, known, and knowledge have disappeared," said Sat. "You have already been shown several techniques, such as the silence between the chants of guru-om, or the gap between one thought and another. I will instruct you further in this field."

Nivritti sat in his meditative posture next to Sat in the hut. A few feet in front of him was a small glass jar about six inches high. There were a few whitish stains on the otherwise clear glass and it looked as if it may have been used to store rice or other foodstuff in the past, but was now empty.

Sat instructed him. "Gaze at the jar. Now imagine the zero point at your Ajna chakra in the middle of your forehead. Count your inhalation of one, one, one towards the jar. Suspend your breath as two, two, two in the jar itself. Then exhale back to the Ajna point as three, three, three. Suspend your breath again at Ajna counting four, four, four. Then count zero and start the breathing cycle again. Make sure the inhalation of your breath, that is, the one, one, one count, is slower than the rest of the cycle. Now gradually decelerate the counts to one, one, two, two and so on. Now, feel your consciousness being absorbed into the jar at the suspension point."

Nivritti did as instructed, and over several minutes gradually decelerated his count. He could feel his consciousness slowly manifesting in the jar space.

Sat sensed Nivritti's state and instructed further, "Now imagine the jar as being completely void of anything."

Nivritti complied and felt himself slowly vanish. There was total stillness and silence.

Whether a few minutes passed or an eternity, Nivritti did not know, for he was in the Shunya. In an instant he found himself again gazing at the jar. He realized that the Shunya could not be described or explained in words. Only the experience of it would allow understanding.

Sat continued. "Gaze at the ground two feet in front of you. Try not to focus your gaze on anything in particular. Keep the concentration of your mind at the tip of your nose. Hold that for a few minutes until you feel your mind relax. Then close your eyes and focus your gaze one inch above the tip of your nose." Nivritti followed these instructions. He maintained his gaze at the ground while concentrating his conscious mind at the tip of his nose. Several minutes passed and he could sense that his mind was still. No extraneous thoughts crept in. He suddenly closed his eyes and concentrated one inch above the tip of his nose. In an instant his inner vision was engulfed in a sea of dark red, as if he were viewing a field of lava before his eyes. All the time his mind maintained its silence. He held the inner vision of the lava field for several minutes and it gradually faded away. "The redness is how you 'perceive' the void in this technique. It is where the sun and moon do not shine, nor does fire light the space. Up to the point of the Ajna chakra, awareness is illumined by the Pingula, Ida, and Sushumna. The Pingula and Ida represent the two channels running in a spiral along the central channel in the spine, the Sushumna. The Kundalini runs along these channels and during meditation runs up the central Sushumna. The Pingula represents the sun, the Ida is the moon, and the Sushumna is fire. These channels end at the Ajna chakra.

Therefore when the yogi ascends beyond this point he must cross the dark-less dark to reach the lightless light," said Sat.

The two sat silently gazing at each other as Nivritti absorbed the words of Sat.

"Let us take a walk," said Sat.

Nivritti followed Sat as they left the village and walked up a small hillside. From the top of the hillside Nivritti could just see the edge of the village and the various groves of mango trees and sugar cane plantations quilting the valley. In the far distance he could make out the peaks of several small mountains.

He and Sat rested at the top of the hill and sat in padmasan gazing across the vista.

Following Sat's instructions, Nivritti placed the tip of index finger to the tip of his thumb and adopted a meditative posture.

"Gaze at the mountain peak and take in the beauty of creation," said Sat.

Nivritti gazed at the scene and felt the exhilaration of nature.

"Remember, Nivritti, that the Pure consciousness is most discernible in the silence, in the suspension point between the breaths. At the point of zero movement of any kind," said Sat.

"Gaze at the distant mountain tops and imagine an invisible line connecting them to your Ajna chakra. On that line write the word ZERO with the Z at the mountain tops and the O in your forehead. Now spell Z, E, R, and O as you move your consciousness along that line. Now delete the O and just move it along Z, E, R. Now slowly drop the R, so you have just Z and E. Now drop the E. Now only the Z remains. Drop that also," said Sat.

Nivritti concentrated his gaze at the mountain top and gradually reduced the ZERO till there was nothing left. As he dissolved the Z he felt himself absorbed into the scene. There was no scene, no mountains, no sky, no Nivritti. He had entered the Shunya.

They returned to the village and Nivritti thanked Sat, Chit, and Ananda for the knowledge and insight they had bestowed on him. He took his leave of them and continued his journey.

Shabdha Guru

Nivritti continued his journey with confidence, knowing that he was on the right path. He had experienced so much in the past few weeks and felt that for the first time in his life he was getting closer to God and the truth.

He had now come to the edge of the forest and ahead he could see an arid landscape of sand with numerous hilly dunes outlining the horizon. He wondered how long they would go on and whether he should turn back. If he got stranded or lost in the desert, or worse still ran out of water, it would not be a good end to his trip. He checked his water pot and it was full. It would be enough to last him a day at the most. He could not decide whether to continue his journey or head back through the jungle. He knew he had not yet met all the seven sages so far.

He sat contemplating what to do and decided to silence his thoughts. As he did so an inner urge to continue across the dunes appeared. He was not sure if it had occurred as a thought but it seemed to appear from the silence. Was it intuitive knowledge coming to him in the silence?

There was only one way to find out. He picked up his pack and water and headed out across the dunes.

Several hours had passed and the sweltering sun was baking Nivritti. He had drunk all his water and could feel the dry blistering of the heat on his lips and cheeks. The heat had created a mirage-like effect and he thought he could see water in the distance. He felt as if he could taste it on his lips, cool and refreshing. High above, the blue sky looked on. The sand was now everywhere, in his clothes and sandals, even stuck to the sweat on his face. It had caked itself onto his skin where it had been roasted in the sun.

He felt so tired. Ahead he thought he could see an oasis — or perhaps this was also a mirage. He picked up his pace with a certain desperation, knowing that if he did not find water soon then the truth was going to be revealed to him sooner than he wanted and not in the way he had imagined it.

As he neared the oasis he felt the fatigue in his limbs. Each step now felt like he were moving an enormous weight. His mind also was a little foggy and he willed himself to get to the water. Several hundred yards from the oasis he fell to his knees, unable to take another step. "I need to rest for a few minutes before I continue," was his final thought as he lay down and closed his eyes.

Nivritti felt someone moving him, could feel someone's arms under his own, dragging him along in the sand. He tried to open his eyes and could make out a figure against the bright sun. He closed his eyes again and rested them in sleep.

Nivritti opened his eyes to a cool breeze across his face and saw the ceiling of a large tent. The canvas was a dark whitish material and he could see the stitching holding it together. He turned his head and looked around the tent. It was quite spacious, at least twenty feet across and tall enough to stand in. He was lying on a cot covered in a woven cotton sheet with an elephant design on it. Black lines with threads of white and orange made up the elephant's body and trunk. He looked closer at it and saw that it was a batik, a common form of ornate painting, glorifying the cotton. It was common in these parts, usually painted by the hand of an unrecognized artist.

He caught a whiff of incense burning and saw the small, thin smoke slowly rising from an incense stick, merging with a faint haze of smoke hovering below the roof of the tent.

A man was sitting in the corner and pouring some water from a large earthen pot into a smaller one. Nivritti was suddenly aware of the dryness of his tongue and mouth.

"You must be very thirsty, young man," said the stranger. "Lucky I found you."

The man turned around, holding the smaller pot. Nivritti was taken a little off guard and could feel himself pull back with a little jerk. The man was in his sixties, with a short grey beard, but most striking of all were his eyes. They were completely white, with no pupils. A blind man in the desert was not something Nivritti was expecting.

Nivritti spent a day or so recovering in the tent. Then a rain storm appeared and it poured for another day. Where was the rain when he had needed it, thought Nivritti. As the storm subsided Nivritti gazed out across the damp desert sand and saw a giant rainbow with its myriad of colors. It was shaped like a large cosmic bow and in his mind Nivritti imagined the archer firing arrows of light and color.

The blind man was Shabha guru, or the guru of words, and he lived by the oasis in the desert. Nivritti could not help but notice that despite the old guru's obvious blindness, he seemed to handle objects and get around no differently than sighted people.

That afternoon Nivritti and Shabdha guru sat together and talked.

"Words are like the mirror to the blind man," said the guru. "Words have allowed me to 'see' things with name and form and also have allowed me to reflect on Pure knowledge.

"Words are not sound, Nivritti, they are sound with meaning. It is from the silence that words and sound emerge," continued the old man. "Words have allowed you not only to function and communicate in your worldly life, but have acted as pointers to the nature of true knowledge on your spiritual search.

"They are invaluable in the realm of relative knowledge and can dispel relative ignorance.

"In this world you will meet many people who have dined on words of knowledge and have bloated egos. They think that scriptural words and phrases are the truth when in fact they are only a reflection of it. Their learning and ego have taken them further away from the truth. One must be always wary of one's ego on this path. The Truth is only revealed to the humble."

"Do not words help to dispel ignorance, oh great guru?" asked Nivritti.

The old sage gestured towards an old gas lamp in the corner of the tent.

"Nivritti, please light the lamp and take it outside," instructed the guru.

Nivritti complied with the request and took the lamp outside. It was late afternoon and the waning sun shone bright into Nivritti's face. From inside the tent the old man called out, "Now, can you see any clearer? Does the light of the lamp help you in the realm of the sun?"

Nivritti looked down at the lamp bathed in the sunlight and could barely see the lit kerosene.

He walked back inside.

"If you were to take your lamp into a dark room to remove the darkness itself you would see that there was no darkness to remove. In the presence of the light there is no such thing as darkness," said the sage.

As Nivritti stood in the doorway he was silhouetted by the sun, casting a long shadow across the tent.

The sage pointed to the ground at Nivritti's shadow.

"Your shadow is there but it is not an object to touch or feel," said the old man as he gestured for Nivritti to move across the tent. Nivritti was no longer in the sunlight and his shadow vanished. "Now your shadow is absent. There is no difference between its presence and its absence, because it does not truly exist," continued the sage.

"I cannot cut your shadow with a sword, as hard as I might try. It is the same with ignorance. In the realm of Pure knowledge there is no ignorance and words cannot therefore remove something that does not truly exist. Using words to know the Truth is like using the light of the lamp to see in the presence of the sun."

"But I feel I am ignorant, oh great sage," protested Nivritti.

The sage paused and gazed at Nivritti.

"In the world of relative knowledge there is ignorance. If one changes one's perspective to the absolute then one realizes that the ignorance is like blue sky where it appears to be reality but is only false since the sky has no color. Or like the imaginary rainbow being an actual bow, or the water from a mirage being able to quench one's thirst.

"To traverse the worldly life one has to change one's perspective from the relative to the Absolute. Only then is it possible to achieve true realization of the Self. As you progress on the spiritual path you will find words very useful, yet ultimately they are of no value in establishing the final Truth. You cannot see the eyes using the eyes. Similarly, the Self cannot know the Self. Only when words have come to an end, and one is basking in the silence, will the Truth be revealed," said the sage.

"True knowledge is when the knower, the object to be known and the knowledge itself are one.

"Where is the truth to be found?" asked Nivritti.

"Where there is 'knowingness' without a knower or an object to be known, then one has reached near the Absolute. Once the knowingness is dissolved, then the highest state of union with the divine is attained. This is Nirvikalpa Samadhi, where there is no longer the seeker attaining the realization of the Self. Where, as in deep sleep, only sentiency remains."

"Is it, then, like a state of deep sleep?" enquired Nivritti.

"No, the yogi is awake and living in the world. He can at will live as the knower of the knowledge, but at other times withdraw into the quietness of his mind and while his eyes are open perform the act of seeing with no seer and no seen object. He is the witnessing consciousness.

"When he chooses he can withdraw also from this 'knowingness' aspect and have only sentiency," replied the sage as he sat quietly.

"I am Shabdha guru, the guru of words, and that, Nivritti, is why I am blind."

The old man smiled at Nivritti and Nivritti gazed silently into the whiteness of the old sage's eyes.

Ajnana- Ignorance

Once he had fully recovered, Nivritti took his leave of the blind sage and headed back across the desert. After a distance he gazed back and could see the oasis as a hazy reflection on the horizon. He stood and watched it for several minutes as it seemed to vanish from his view. Was the oasis and its blind guru just a mirage like words themselves? he wondered.

After a day of travelling back across the desert he reached a lightly wooded area with a small creek running through it. He decided to follow the creek. Ahead he could see it joining a larger river and watched the water of the slow-flowing creek merging with the larger river, creating small ripples of disturbance as the creek was absorbed into the faster-flowing water.

Nearby were some jackfruit trees. He picked a jackfruit and sat under the tree to eat the sweet fruit. His snack completed, he leaned his head back against the tree and relaxed, pondering his journey so far. His eyelids felt heavy as he closed his eyes.

He opened his eyes to a splashing noise. In the river he could see a man standing at the confluence of the creek and river, his hands in the water, pushing some of the water in one direction. Nivritti watched the man's futile action.

"What are you doing?" called Nivritti.

"I am trying to keep the water from the creek separate from the river water, but it's tough going," said the man.

"I come here every day and do the same thing.

"My name is Ajnana, by the way. What's yours?"

"I am Nivritti, I am journeying to see the sages in the forest so I may come to know the truth," said Nivritti.

"Yes, yes, we get many seekers coming through here looking for that," said Ajnana.

"I know the truth," he said nonchalantly as he gazed back into the water and continued his task.

"I have read all the great spiritual works, the Bhagavad Gita, the Upanishads, the Bible, all of them, and I know their true meaning. I can teach it to you sometime if you like."

"Oh, that would be great," said Nivritti hesitantly.

"Right now, though, I have to put the fish that I have created back into the creek," said Ajnana as he waded back across the river towards Nivritti. He knelt down on the river bank a few meters from Nivritti and carefully opened up a cloth package. Nivritti walked over and stood behind Ajnana. Inside were beautifully sculpted fish that appeared to be shaped out of a whitish material.

"Wow, those are very good fish, did you make them yourself?" asked Nivritti.

"Yes," said Ajnana. "It took me a lot of time and effort to carve the shape of the fish exactly, but the trickiest bit was getting the salt to stick together in a fish shape without falling apart."

"The fish are made out of salt?" said Nivritti, amazed and a little taken aback.

"Of course," said Ajnana.

"What are you going to do with your fish?" asked Nivritti.

Ajnana turned his head slightly and gazed back at Nivritti out of one eye.

"I am going to put them in the river, of course, because that is where fish live!" said Ajnana as if Nivritti were asking a foolish question.

"I can't keep them on the land because fish live in the water," he added with a hint of condescension.

He carefully picked up one salt fish in each hand and waded a few feet into the creek. His hands descended under the water and as they did so the fish dissolved and were merged into the water.

"Darn it!" exclaimed Ajnana. "That happens every time. But mark my words, one of these days one of my salt fish are gonna swim away."

Ajnana walked back to the shore and shook his hands to dry them off. He was a stocky man, probably in his thirties, wearing khaki shorts and a white t-shirt. He gestured past Nivritti to the jackfruit trees.

"You didn't eat one of those jackfruits, did you?" he asked.

"Yes, they are delicious. Do you want one?" asked Nivritti.

"No, no," said Ajnana. "There is a poisonous snake on that tree so I never go near it. You're lucky you didn't get bitten by it."

Ajnana pointed back to the jackfruit tree. Several feet above where Nivritti had been sitting there appeared to be a snake coiled several times around a branch.

Nivritti could not make it out clearly and he walked back towards the tree to get a closer look.

"Don't be a fool!" exclaimed Ajnana. "It's poisonous and will bite you."

Ignoring Ajnana, Nivritti approached the tree slowly. As he came closer he could see a dark black object wrapped several times around the branch. It was not a snake but a piece of old dirty rope. He gave a sigh of relief.

"It's only a piece of old rope," Nivritti called back to Ajnana without turning around.

"Doesn't matter what you say, I am not risking getting bitten by a snake for some jackfruit, doesn't matter how tasty they are," said Ajnana.

Nivritti turned back and looked at Ajnana, who was now busily rolling up the cotton in which his salt fish had been wrapped. He was not like the other people he had met on the journey so far, in fact, he seemed far more like the people he knew back in his village. He was someone living the worldly life, or Samsara, the world full of opposites like happiness and sadness, gain and loss, except now Nivritti could see the futility in Ajnana's actions. He realized that he would have been just like Ajnana had he not made this journey, and that if he were not always vigilant there was a risk of falling back from the spiritual path to the world of ignorance. He would have to guard against arrogance and the feeling of superiority that befalls the spiritual seeker. The idea that one possesses knowledge that others do not, that it somehow confers an intimacy to the divine that others lack, these were pitfalls to be avoided. Only by true humility and ultimately sacrificing one's individuality on the altar of love and devotion would the goal be reached. As these thoughts crossed his mind he heard a voice.

"Nivritti, wake up."

Nivritti opened his eyes. He was sitting under the jackfruit tree, and in front of him was standing his guru, Gahnininath. He looked around. The creek and river were as before, but there was no sign of Ajnana.

"Ajnana was here in your dream. In the world of pure knowledge, ignorance cannot exist," said the guru. "Nivritti, it is time for you to return to your worldly life."

"Guruji, is my journey over?" asked Nivritti.

"Nivritti, there is no journey, no path, no goal to be reached. There is only the Truth. It requires no other qualification," said the guru.

"You have visited the sages and they have guided you in the ways of the Truth.

"The world is not created by the Lord in order to see his creation. It just is. It manifests because that is the nature of the divine. You are like the wave on the ocean, living the life of the unenlightened. The emphasis is on the wave and how it is born, lives out its brief existence, and then is gone. Importance is given to this and also to the other waves that one sees. Spiritual unfolding occurs by changing the viewpoint and realizing that all the waves are ultimately water and exist in the vast ocean. In the realm of the ocean the wave is unimportant. When one reaches into the ocean to pick up a wave, all that remains in one's hand is the water. Or it is like seeing the sun of pure consciousness providing lightness or darkness when the reality is that the sun provides neither. The sunlight itself is dark and cannot be seen and only in its reflection are light and dark of any importance. The sun shines irrespective of the perceived lightness and darkness.

"Similarly, one's own existence in the three states is also the illusion. It is the underlying 'I' of these three states that is the reality. In one's thoughts, when one looks at the flower one sees the object and knows it to be a flower. The reality is that the knower of the flower, the knowing and the flower itself are really the same 'I' manifesting at different points. The eye of the eye, the ear of the ear, and the mind of the mind is where the Truth resides. The seer viewing himself in the mirror sees himself. The subject and the object are the same and there is only the process of seeing. When you return you must try and maintain this view of the world, that all you see around you is nothing but divine manifestation. The world is as it should be. It is perfect in every way. Any other viewpoint is giving unnecessary importance to the individuality and leads to the knower/known duality that is the seat of ignorance.

"This knowledge cannot be taught or learnt or known by any means. Words have little value in revealing it. It is to be found in silence. One's thoughts seem like they run continuously but that is not the reality. The silence between one thought and the next, where the knower/known difference has not yet begun, is where Pure knowledge can be found.

"Anywhere in the world where there is a transition point is called Yoga Bhumika. It is the gap between two thoughts, the gap between day and night or inside and outside, the sleeping and awake states. That is where one must focus one's attention to find the Truth.

"It is there in the silence that the Lord's voice can be heard most clearly.

"Continue your meditation and always try and maintain this view of the world. Only by the yogi's constant vigilance and effort can enlightenment be reached. Once you are close, then all efforts to read or study this subject must be dropped. Then one can dwell in effortless existence, with the mind withdrawn from the senses, thereby living life with no knower or knowledge to be known. Only knowingness, and ultimately withdrawing this also until only sentiency alone remains."

"Guruji, having dropped all methods of attaining and understanding knowledge such as words, mind, and intellect, how will I know the Truth?" asked Nivritti.

"I do not know, but I will tell you what my own guru told me: The one who thinks he does not know, he alone knows."

Nivritti gazed at his guru and knew the truth of his words. Behind the guru he could see the river. It grew bigger and bigger as he watched. The waves gushed higher and higher. In the water Nivritti could see all of human existence. He could see desire, loss, pain, anger, hatred, and all the aspects of worldly existence manifest in the raging water.

"That is the river of Samsara, or worldly existence," said the guru as the noise of the torrential flow increased.

"You will have to cross it to get back."

Nivritti was petrified. He would surely drown in those waters. He gazed up at his guru.

The guru smiled. "Take my hand and I will guide you," he said.

Nivritti grasped his guru's hand and they headed to the water's edge. The river was now at least a hundred feet across with huge ten foot waves and foam swirling all around.

The guru started across the water and Nivritti followed. Nivritti could see that both he and the guru were able to walk across the water without sinking, but nevertheless the waves lashed up across their feet and soaked their clothes.

They continued across, and as Nivritti looked down into the water he made out all the miseries of human life. He could see birth and death and sorrow. Millions of people were there, all crying out in their misery. He looked up at the guru as if to ask whether they could stop and help these people. His fear overcame him and he silently gripped the guru's hand even tighter.

As they neared the other side he felt his grip start to slip from the guru's hand and knew he was about to fall into the vast river of Samsara. Terrified he cried out, "Guruji, save me!"

"Jump, Nivritti, jump!" shouted the guru.

Nivritti closed his eyes and leapt as hard as could. He felt himself soaring through the air and his feet hit sand. He fell forward onto the dry sand and breathed a sigh of relief. He turned around to make sure the guru had made it and gasped.

Behind him was only sand, a dried-up river bed where the raging water had been. The river of Samsara was gone, as was the guru.

Jivan Mukta- The liberated Soul

Nivritti returned to his village and resumed his life as before, yet he was different. He sensed it in himself and others noticed the difference, too. It was not that he was now somehow immune to the events of his life, but that the same events did not shake the underlying tranquility that he had obtained on his journey.

His elderly uncle Bapu died several weeks after Nivritti's return and he stood at the funeral pyre holding Rukmini's frail hand. He felt the sadness at his uncle's loss and gazed around at the sad faces of all the mourners that had gathered to send off the poet-mailman.

The Hindu priest was busily reciting mantras and stotras from ancient works that constituted the last rites. As he stood in his grief he internally counted his breath from his Anhaat chakra up to his Ajna chakra. This had become his main form of meditation since his return. Slowly his breath stilled, as did his mind. Underlying his grief he could sense the intense bliss, or Ananda, rising within him until his grief was totally engulfed in it. There was no sorrow here, no loss, no feeling that he would never see his uncle again, or hold his hand or take him to worship at Brahmana. The only reality was the bliss. It underlay everything.

After the funeral he had gone to Brahmana, Bapu's temple, and had stood silently in the cathedral of the banyan tree. There he could feel the intense vibrations within his body as he entered the arches and knew that it was the Chaitanya of the old buried sage.

Every so often he would feel his anger rising. It made his mind focused and one-pointed. He contemplated its nature. No judgement of it, no reasoning it out. Thus doing, it too would dissolve in a sea of blissfulness.

When riding past the crematorium he no longer felt the fear and heartache that had gripped him before. Instead he saw the ash covering the sun and the dark orange glow it created. He pondered that despite the fact that the ash cloud was blocking out the sun, it was visible only because of the light of the sun itself.

One morning as he and Janesh were cycling into Sarabagh for their work, he had an intuitive urge to stop and buy some jillibee. The thought arose spontaneously from his silence. He gestured for Janesh to pull over at the Mithai store that sold all sorts of sweet delights. He purchased the sticky, sweet orange jillibees wrapped in newspaper and continued on to the dhobiwala's shop. As they neared the store he could see the irritating old beggar, although now the old man's jibes no longer bothered him.

"Where is my Dakshina, Nivritti?" called the old beggar.

Nivritti pulled up, got off his bike, and leaned it against the wall next to the old man.

"What dakshina would you like, old beggar?" asked Nivritti.

The old beggar smiled and Nivritti could see his rotten black teeth.

"Jillibee, go and get me some jillibee," cried the old beggar.

"Here you go," said Nivritti as he handed the beggar the package of jillibee wrapped in the newspaper.

The beggar was startled for an instant, then grabbed the newspaper. He tore it open and proceeded to devour the jillibee, the orange syrup creating a stain around his mouth.

As Nivritti watched the beggar he was filled with an inexplicable joy. He gazed upon the form of the beggar busily eating the sweets and could feel the same form appear in his Anahaat chakra in the center of his heart. The form began to change and he recognized the outline of Lord Shiva that he had seen. The form of Shiva was now the external vison of the beggar, and the internal vision as well. The form changed again and the form of his beloved guru Gahininath appeared.

The guru looked up at him from the jillibee.

"The guru manifests everywhere as Lord Shiva, as the external physical guru with name and form, and also as the guru within you, the Sad-guru," said Gahininath.

"Comprehending this is part of realizing the Truth. Continue on your path, Nivritti. Always keep the form of the Lord in your heart. All things around you are manifestations of the same divine form. Keep your mind still, live your life guided by inner intuition. The inner Pure knowledge will guide you. God is Jnana. When you see the blue pearl of pure consciousness in your inner vision, then your journey will be at an end," said the guru.

The guru slowly faded away from his vision and Nivritti watched the old beggar finish his treat and then turned and walked his bike to work.

His best friend Jnanesh had also noticed the change in Nivritti. Although on the outside Nivritti was the same friend he had always known, there was something different about him. It was not new airs, as if he was showing off some knowledge of enlightenment that he had obtained. It was difficult to pinpoint exactly, but he had a serenity about him that had not been there previously. The anger within him had also gone. Jnanesh wanted to know if he could also obtain some of Nivritti's newfound tranquility. Nivritti had described the journey to him and he had listened in awe at the stories of the old ruined temple, the tiger, and meeting the various sages and gurus along the path. He knew that he was not the kind of person to undertake such an endeavor.

One evening, as he sat with Nivritti at his house, he mustered up the courage to ask him.

"Nivritti, I want to know what you know. I want to know God," he said.

"Oh," said Nivritti. He had always assumed Jnanesh was content in the practice of worship and devotion.

"You can continue on the spiritual path you are on, Jnanesh, it will lead you to a state of enlightenment," said Nivritti.

"I know, but I want you to teach me the path you have followed," said Jnanesh.

An intuitive urge to go to Brahmana arose in Nivritti.

"OK, let's go to Brahmana," said Nivritti.

The two friends walked across the paddy fields to the old banyan cathedral.

"How come you never use your full name, Jnanesh?" said Nivritti.

Jnanesh laughed and said, "Only my mother and some old aunties call me by my full name."

"Jnaneshwar, I like it better," said Nivritti.

"Yes, auntie!" said Jnanesh and the two friends laughed as they made their way into the cathedral.

In the cathedral the two sat across from one another in padmasan.

Nivritti stilled his mind. He could feel the intense Chaitanya rising within himself and all around.

Then, Nivritti initiated Jnaneshwar onto the
path.

Author Biography

Milind Dhond is a cardiologist practicing in Northern California. He has practiced kundalini yoga under the direction of Swami Radhikananda Saraswati for the last fifteen years. He currently resides in Davis, California. He is a Professor at UC Davis, a sixth degree black belt and Professor of Dan Zan Ryu Jujitsu. He is the sensei of Green Valley Kodenkan where he teaches Jujitsu and Kundalini yoga. He is the author of over fifty medical books and papers. He has previously published *Journey to Zero* which is an interpretation of Vijnana Bhairava, an 8th century yoga text with 112 techniques for achieving states of enlightenment

www.ingramcontent.com/pod-product-compliance
Lightning Source LLC
Chambersburg PA
CBHW070206060426
42445CB00033B/1608